Art &
Sole

LAURENCE KING

Published in 2008 by
Laurence King Publishing Ltd.
361–373 City Road
London EC1V 1JJ
United Kingdom
enquiries@laurenceking.co.uk
www.laurenceking.co.uk

Intercity ♣

Copyright © text and design 2008 Intercity
www.intercitydesign.com

Cover art by Dave White.

A catalogue record for this book is available from
the British Library.

ISBN: 978 185669 565 7

Printed in China.

Art & Sole

Contemporary Sneaker Art & Design

Written & Designed by Intercity

Contents

It all started with sport; and the sport that's done most to propel the humble sneaker to its current celebrity status is basketball. In the 1970s, the only basketball shoes available to the US public came in relatively standard colours such as white, black or navy blue. This made the team-coloured sneakers worn on professional basketball courts, which were often produced to match team strips, very sought after. In those days, colour was just as important as brand name, if not more so. Sneakers defined who you were and, much the same as today, wearing sneakers that no one else had was the main concern.

The mid-1970s saw the dawning of hip-hop culture, and with it a new-found attitude to the wearing of sneakers. Previously, sneakers were worn on the world's streets and basketball courts for both style and function (the more beat-up the shoe, the better the basketball player), but the advent of b-boy culture saw them being worn purely for style. Sneakers were now being preserved in pristine condition for that all-important fresh-out-of-the-box look — and rising prices also ensured that looking after your sneakers guaranteed getting your money's worth. This trend was seen the world over; whether sneakers were initially worn for skateboarding, playing football or just wandering the streets, it was hip-hop culture that turned them into objects of desire. Just think back to Run-DMC's 'Walk This Way' promo; it's a much-cited example, but those box-fresh adidas Superstars had a lasting impact on the youth culture of the day.

Permanently associated with creative subcultures such as hip-hop and skateboarding (both of which have a strong history of customizing shoes), the sneaker scene has always been connected with creativity and this book sets out to document the current state of this relationship. The book is split into two halves: the first half displays the collaborative and limited-edition sneakers produced by a wide range of artists and designers; and the second documents the burgeoning art scene connected with this phenomenon. The work featured in the second section of the book emphasizes the iconic nature of the sneaker; from Dave White's expressionist oil paintings (see page 130) to Shin Tanaka's beautiful origami sneakers (see page 136), and even sculptures made from the shoes themselves, the work draws its inspiration from an object that has become fetishized by many.

The creative side of the sneaker scene has made the artist or designer collaboration an obvious alliance, creating a phenomenon that has grown rapidly since the beginning of the twenty-first century. The results are often limited-edition, highly collectable sneakers featuring premium fabrics, unique colourways and bespoke packaging. These are not always shoes you can find in your local sneaker store; if you want to acquire them you have to be knowledgeable, dedicated (overnight queuing is often required) and sometimes well connected. The limited nature of some of these releases can create sneakers with a near-mythical status, like the Nike DUNKLE Low on page 17, or the JB Classics MÖTUG shoe on page 42. The rarest and most sought-after shoes can skyrocket in value (sometimes within the space of a few weeks) and, as these shoes are often only available in specific locations, they frequently crop up in online auctions with generously inflated price tags. Of course, not all artist/designer collaborations are produced in limited numbers; for great examples of mass-produced sneaker art just look at Staple Design's Nike Navigation Pack (production run of 10,000) or Tattoo Series (production run of 30,000) on page 69.

Researching this book wasn't easy. Apart from the rarity of the sneakers themselves and the fact that (amazingly) most sneaker manufacturers don't keep records of their products, there are so many sneaker collaborations to choose from. Collaborations are currently everywhere, and not just in the world of sneakers — even corporate brands with more traditional marketing strategies are getting in on the act. The results can produce some unseemly team efforts, with 2007's Prada and Carphone Warehouse mobile phone collaboration probably being one of the most ill-fitting. Perhaps unsurprisingly, this has led to collaboration becoming something of a dirty word (along with the term 'limited edition', which applies to almost all products these days). But the fact is, even though the (sneaker) marketplace has become saturated with collaborations, the phenomenon is not going away. Where sports brands once looked to athletes to add credibility and desirability to their products, they now look to artists and designers.

A recent development in the scene has witnessed artists and designers actually influencing the design of sneakers themselves. Just look at +41's hybrid art pieces (combining elements of various sneaker models), which seemed to have spawned a whole new craze in sneaker production (see page 154), or Hiroshi Fujiwara's radical woven creations (see pages 50 and 51). It could be said that there are currently too many releases of retro shoe models, and even the collaborative limited-edition shoes tend to be based on the safety of the manufacturers' best-selling models — a policy that creates obvious limitations. The future of the artist/designer collaboration could well lie in the construction of the actual shoe as well as the choice of artwork, material and colour. In fact, at the time of writing, Crooked Tongues (see pages 38—43) were working on a confidential project with an as-yet-unnamed sneaker manufacturer to create their own shoe, working on all stages of design. Let's hope that this is the shape of things to come in the ever-evolving relationship between art, design and the sneaker.

Intercity

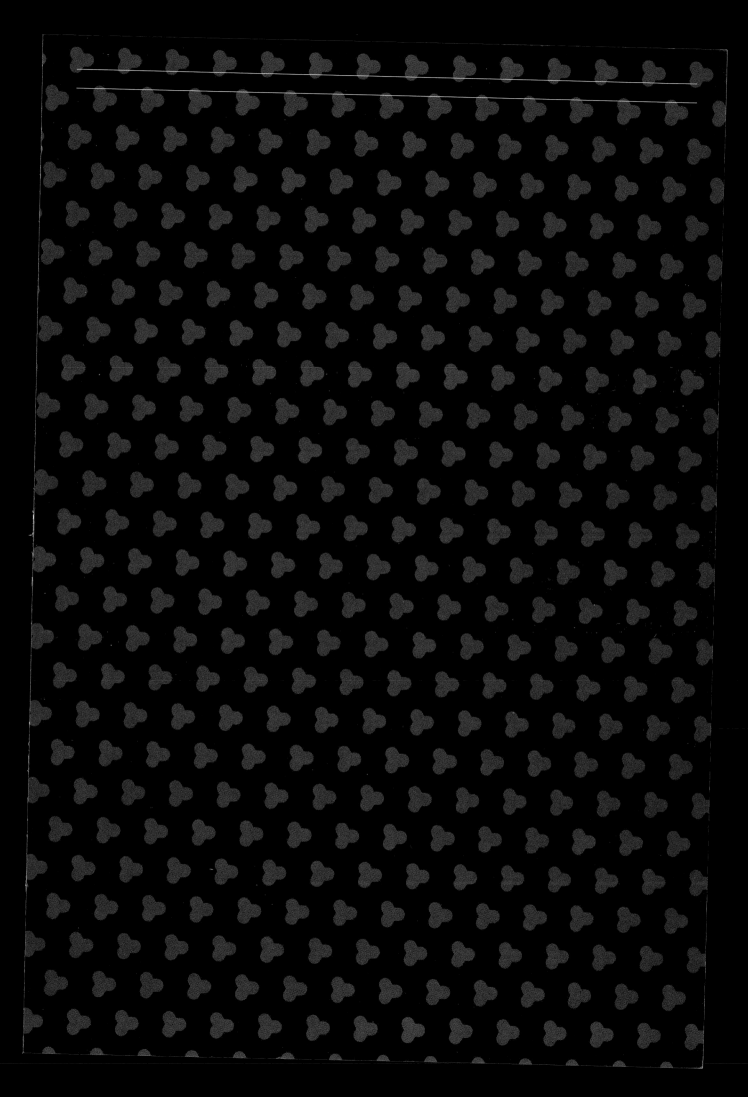

COLLABORATIONS

PROJECTS

Snea
&Art

Art & Makers

KATSUYA TERADA

Prolific Japanese artist Katsuya Terada is probably best known as the character designer for the animated Manga classic *Blood: The Last Vampire*. Terada defines himself as a *rakugaki* artist, a Japanese term for a drawing style and philosophy in which the artist draws continuously without too much thought. He has also worked for US comics such as *Iron Man* and *Hellboy*.

In 2005, Terada applied his art to the Nike Air Zoom Terra Tattoo. The graphics were inspired by the elements air, wind, fire and water, with the right shoe differing from the left as the story of the illustration unfolds across both sneakers. Limited to 300 pairs worldwide, the package also contained a wooden shoebox laser-engraved with Terada's artwork.

VAUGHN BODE

An icon to graffiti writers and an influence on street culture from the mid-1970s to the present day, the late Vaughn Bodé was one of the most influential American cartoonists of our time. In September 1957, Bodé designed Cheech Wizard (shown below) a unique little character who wore a huge yellow hat covered in red and black stars. The inspiration for the name came from an ordinary can of Cheechy nuts.

In 2007 Puma introduced the Vaughn Bodé Clyde to celebrate the 50th anniversary of the creation of this iconic cartoon character. Released in two colourways, the first instalment stayed true to the Cheech Wizard identity, while the second, all-white version sported a much more wearable look. Limited to only 264 pairs in each colourway and made from nubuck leather with high-gloss printed stars, the sneakers feature three sets of laces for colour customization and a key chain explaining the history of Cheech.

Mark Bodé, Vaughn's son and an artist in his own right, teamed up with Puma to design both the sneakers and a Bodé-style hoodie for that all-important match-up.

The original Cheech Wizard character by Vaughn Bodé (below left). Shown below is an original sketch for the Puma Vaughn Bodé Clyde by Mark Bodé. Cheech Wizard is © Mark Bodé 2008.

THE CLYDE

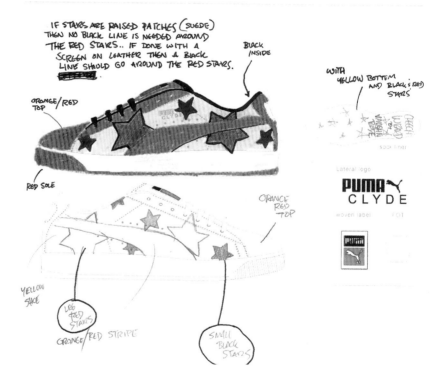

www.thegasface.co.uk

GASIUS

Released as part of a set of shoes bearing the unofficial title of the Capital Series, this Nike Vengeance was designed by London-based Gasius (aka Russell Maurice) in 2005. There were five shoes in the series, one from each of five European capital cities and each designed by a local creative.

The design of this shoe, the GasrNike, is based on the repetition of graffiti and the artist's fascination with the diamond and triangle shapes that are a recurring theme in much of his work. The shoe was a limited edition of 240 pairs. Russell Maurice was also part of the 90x90 art project featured on page 208.

www.unkle.com

UNKLE

The Nike Dunk High SB UNKLE, aka the DUNKLE, was one of the biggest releases of 2004. The project was a collaboration between UK-based DJ James Lavelle – founder of record label Mo' Wax and recording act UNKLE, New York graffiti legend Futura 2000 and art director/designer Ben Drury. Each had previously produced artwork for a number of Mo' Wax record sleeves and had been instrumental in defining the imagery of UNKLE's unique aesthetic.

Featuring Futura's famous Pointman and Atmos artwork, the shoes use a combination of leather and nubuck, with a patent leather swoosh. A total of 11 different screens were used to achieve the print effect.

It is rumoured that there are only five pairs of the low-top version in existence. They were made for Lavelle's friends and family only.

THE HAÇIENDA

To celebrate the 25th anniversary of legendary Manchester nightclub The Haçienda, Factory Records teamed up with Y-3 (the brand created by adidas and fashion designer Yohji Yamamoto) to create FAC51-Y3. The project is a collaboration between Peter Saville (the original graphic designer for Factory records and some-time collaborator with Yohji Yamamoto), Ben Kelly (architect for the Haçienda) and Peter Hook (bass player for Joy Division/New Order).

Based on the classic Y-3 Sprint, the shoes are enclosed in a unique six-sided maple-bottomed shoebox inspired by the shape of the club's dance floor. Within the box, the shoes come wrapped in four sheets of tissue paper; two featuring Kevin Cummins' photography of the club in its 1980s heyday, one showing Ben Kelly's original sketches for the club's interior and one reflecting how the space looks today.

A DVD is also included in the box, featuring original footage from the club and a discussion between Saville, Kelly and Hook about the project and their memories of the Haçienda. Retailing at £345, the shoes were limited to just 250 pairs worldwide.

Every release from Factory Records was given a FAC number; the name FAC51-Y3 expresses the co-operation between the Haçienda (FAC51) and Y-3. Shown above is a pair of FAC51-Y3s sitting on an original metal plate from the Haçienda's pillars, with pieces of wood from the original dance floor.

www.irakny.com

IRAK NY

IRAK NY began as a graffiti crew in New York City in the mid-1990s, and over the years has developed into a clothing line, establishing the brand as a creative outlet for its members.

In 2007, adidas joined forces with IRAK NY for their first collaboration, using the Torsion model as the canvas for their design. The sneaker features a fresh retro colourway, using a grey upper with black, blue, neon yellow and hot red accents.

The Torsion was the model of choice again in 2008 for a second collaboration, this time featuring beautiful orange suede, a purple tongue and green accents. Both sneakers feature the word 'IRAK' with the year date on the toe, and only 300 pairs of each model were produced.

www.akanyc.com

ALSO KNOWN AS

Inspired by vintage spray paint colours, Also Known As (AKA) created this collection of seven patent leather Nike Dunk Lows in collaboration with Nike iD. Five sets of the shoes were produced, none of which were made available at retail. One of the five sets, however, was auctioned via eBay, with all proceeds going to the Free Arts NYC, a non-profit organization dedicated to bringing the healing and therapeutic powers of the arts into the lives of abused and neglected children and their families. The final bid was placed at US$14,900, making the price of each Dunk US$2128.57.

AKA also created these limited laser-etched Nike Air Force 1's (shown opposite, top right) for the release of the Also Known As book by 12ozProphet in 2005. The shoes were designed by Allen Benedikt of AKA, with handstyles by Crude Oil, and hand lasering by Tom Luedecke at Nike's fabled Innovation Kitchen in Beaverton, Oregon. There were just under 50 pairs produced and all were given away to a carefully crafted list of friends, collaborators and celebrities. Each pair came with the extra-rare gold covered edition of *Also Known As*, volume one.

The NB AVENJ is a collaboration between New Balance and Sean D'Anconia of Canadian new-media design group Her Majesty's Secret Studio. Part of the New Balance 574 Artist Series, and launched in tandem with HMSS menswear collection AVENJ, the shoe pays homage to 1970s grindhouse cinema. The artwork features a collage of icons from the era, including skyscrapers of Hong Kong, the streets of Harlem and references to the Yakuza and Kung Fu. The canary-yellow colour of the shoe was chosen as a tribute to Bruce Lee's unfinished Kung Fu epic *Game of Death*.

The detailing in this shoe is amazing; for example, the Afro hairstyle on faux blaxploitation star Kujo Yamato is actually made from a flocked fabric. Other unique design features include raised scales on the dragon-themed tattoo art, while the signature 'N' is made from luminescent material.

The NB AVENJ was also available as a deluxe package featuring signed and numbered shoes, a T-shirt and a limited-edition lithograph.

www.majestysecret.com

SEAN D'ANCONIA

www.joshwisdumb.com

JOSH WISDUMB

Abstract artist Josh 'Wisdumb' Spivack got together with New Balance to design this limited-edition 574, with Wisdumb's black and white line work being rubber-etched on to the white leather upper. An underrated design, this sneaker was largely miscredited to Eric Haze. This was due to the fact that the colourway of the shoe was similar to an existing Haze collaboration (see page 24), and Wisdumb was not properly credited when the shoe was first released, Haze was wrongly assumed to be the designer.

NIKE DUNK – THE HAZE PROJECT

In 2003, working with Nike design director Jesse Leyva, Haze produced these Dunks (High and Low) inspired by his graffiti style. The vignettes were created with the use of an airbrush, meaning each shoe was one of a kind. A special version of the shoe (with a Haze embroidered tongue label and special Haze box) was limited to an edition of 250 and distributed through an online raffle in Los Angeles and New York.

www.interhaze.com

HAZE

Eric Haze is a now-legendary graffiti artist from New York. Born in 1961, Haze was part of the collective of artists who first brought graffiti into the arena of art galleries – alongside names such as Keith Haring and Jean-Michel Basquiat. Not only a graffiti artist, Haze founded a graphic design studio in 1984, producing logo designs for the likes of Public Enemy and MTV, as well as album covers for The Beastie Boys (*Check Your Head*) and Tommy B Records.

In 1991, Haze moved to Los Angeles, where alongside his design studio, he founded an independent clothing company named Haze. The company launched a streetwear range featuring the unique drawing and lettering style he had developed as a graffiti writer. The Haze company has also produced limited-edition jewellery, furniture, posters and skateboards. In 2005 Haze relocated back to New York, where he continues to push his product line while also taking part in various art and design projects around the world. Recent collaborations include sneaker designs for both Nike and New Balance, a G-Shock watch for Casio, a Be@rbrick design for Medicom Toys and even a custom show car for Toyota/Scion.

NEW BALANCE 574 HAZE

Haze produced this 574 in 2006 as part of the New Balance Artist Series. Produced in a limited run, the shoe features Haze's trademark black and white drawing style.

www.clawmoney.com

CLAW MONEY

Released in 2007, the limited-edition Nike Claw Blazer was the first of a two-part collaboration between Nike and female graffiti legend Claw Money. The sneakers were released in three colourways and featured Claw Money's signature three-nailed claw symbol, which is based on the letter W.

Later the same year, the anticipated follow-up to the Blazer, the Nike Claw Vandal High, was released. According to Claw, she has a special connection with this sneaker: 'I wanted to do the Vandal because it's my favourite hi-top, and, after all, I'm a vandal, too.'

Claw, who also runs her own clothing label and is fashion editor of *Swindle* magazine, added peacock feathers to the body in reflective ink to achieve a more *couture* look.

www.reconstore.com

STASH

Born in New York, Stash (aka Josh Franklin) started writing graffiti in the stairway of his building in 1980; he painted his last active subway train in 1987. Another of graffiti's elite artists to have made the crossover into the worlds of art and design, Stash has since established himself as an influencer and innovator in the world of clothing design. Founder of legendary clothing studio Subware Visual Maintenance, Stash also collaborated with friend and fellow graffiti artist Futura 2000 on the Project Dragon clothing line and the opening of Recon clothing (with stores in New York, San Francisco and Tokyo). He has also collaborated with many other labels, working as a designer for A Bathing Ape, taking part in the Gravis Superhero Foot bed project (see page 124) and working with Nike on a number of sneaker designs.

NIKE KOBE 24 PREMIUM PACK
Nike and Stash collaborated in 2006 to celebrate Kobe Bryant's 24-hour-a-day dedication to basketball, uniting Bryant's passion for basketball with the culture that surrounds the game. Just 100 sets of the sneakers (and jacket) were released worldwide.

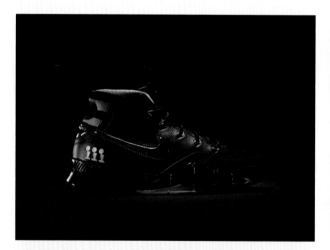

NIKE BLUE PACK

Stash collaborated with Nike on this pack of two sneakers in 2006 – including a Nike Air Max 95 and an Air Force 1 Low IO Premium. Nike also released a hyperstrike version of the Air Force 1; the left shoe featured an embroidered Stash tag and laser-engraved Stash graphic, and the right foot featured an embroidered Futura 2000 tag and laser-engraved Futura 2000 logo. This edition was never released to the public.

NIKE AF-X MID QK

Released in 2004, and featuring a black Recon camouflage pattern, this shoe has a steel toecap and laser-engraved Recon logo. The hyperstrike version again featured a steel toecap and laser-engraved Recon logo, but this time came in an olive Recon camouflage pattern. The shoes also feature a silver strap buckle and Recon logo lace tag.

NIKE DUNK HIGH PREMIUM F2T.50

Made for Futura 2000's 50th birthday in Hawaii, these Nike Dunks are embroidered with F2T.50. The sneakers were given to family and friends only and never released to the public. Futura chose the colour palette, with fabrics chosen by Stash. Released in 2006.

NIKE AIR FORCE 1 HIGH

Released in three cities (Tokyo, New York and London), this shoe came with a different coloured metal box for each city. Individually numbered (different for each city), the shoes were limited to 1250 pairs and feature Stash's Fat Cap graphic. Originally released in 2003, the collaboraton was recently voted the best Air Force 1 make-up in the 25 year history of the shoe.

NIKE PAUL RODRIGUEZ ZOOM AIR ELITE

Released in 2006, this shoe features a laser-engraved Brooklyn skyline.

GRAVIS BLACK BOX
Teaming up for Gravis' limited-release Black Box series in 2006, Stash worked on a line of shoes, luggage, bags and accessories, creating an exclusive purple camouflage. The Gravis Comet Mid shoe (which was also available in white) was part of an international tour (stopping at New York, Los Angeles and Tokyo) to launch the collection.

www.kaiandsunny.com

KAI AND SUNNY

As well as producing work for advertising, publishing, exhibitions, fashion and music clients, illustrators and art directors Kai and Sunny also run their own fashion label, Call Of The Wild.

In 2008, Reebok collaborated with Call Of The Wild to produce this Nightsky Mid-Hiker (a Reebok Nightsky that has been converted into a hiking boot). It comes in two colourways – black/silver and brown/gold – and is made from a mix of leather, corduroy and Gore-tex. It also features a 'kryptonite' print on the lining designed by Kai and Sunny.

According to Kai and Sunny, 'Call Of The Wild has a strong connection to nature, making a hiking model the natural choice for this collaboration.' The boot was limited to only 100 pairs in each colourway.

In 2005 Kai and Sunny also produced this illustration of a Nike Cortez sneaker for the London Nike iD studio.

www.maedastudio.com

JOHN MAEDA

Renowned graphic designer, visual artist, computer scientist and professor (at the Massachusetts Institute of Technology Media Lab), John Maeda continues to push the boundaries of both art and technology. In 2007, Maeda teamed up with Reebok to create this Ventilator Timetanium. Inspired by the personal nature of sneakers, the project explored the mass-produced custom sneaker phenomenon, integrating production technology purely for artistic reasons. Maeda created original mathematic algorithms and computer codes to create the imagery for the shoe; his hand-written code is featured on the insole and lining of the shoe, with the graphic generated from this code displayed on the outer. Limited to only 100 pairs worldwide, the shoes were exclusively available through www.rbkcustom.com, Reebok's custom sneaker website.

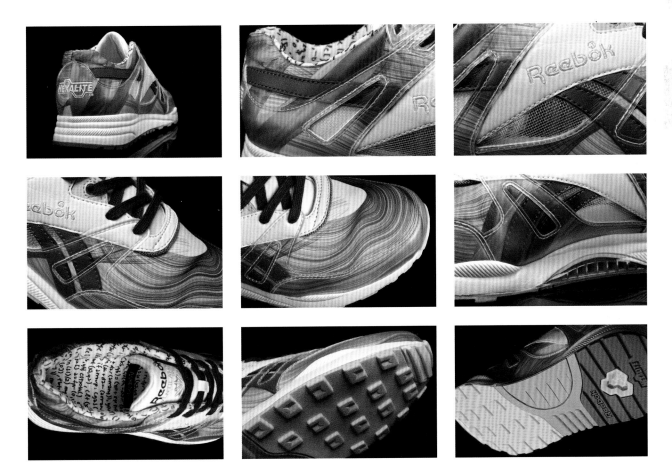

www.kikstyoshop.com

KIKS TYO

KIKS TYO is a Japanese streetwear brand that was founded in 2006 by DJ and designer hobby:tech (aka Shinichi Izaki). Aside from his work with KIKS TYO, hobby:tech is known as one of the founding members of Japanese creative team Brownrats, as a recording artist and DJ for Universal Music Japan and as one of Japan's most prominent sneaker collectors.

In 2007, KIKS TYO teamed up with G-Shock and New Balance to release the co-branded G-Flash series, which was created in celebration of G-Shock's 25th anniversary. The series included two Casio G-Shock watches, two pairs of New Balance 574s and one pair of sleekly modified NB320s.

As part of the project, KIKS TYO produced a range of advertising and T-shirts featuring Japanese bikini model Aki Hoshino.

Online sneaker resource (and store) Crooked Tongues is the public face of London-based creative agency Unorthodox Styles. It was founded in 2000 to address the lack of qualitative information about the sneaker scene – at times the online experience can be fragmented and often unreliable. Crooked Tongues' goal was to gather the elements of value to the sneaker community and create a single online resource.

The website includes news, interviews with key players and in-depth information on upcoming and current releases. There is also the opportunity for users to upload and display their collections, or just show off what they're wearing each day (which always provokes lively debate).

As ardent sneaker enthusiasts, the team at Crooked Tongues has worked on numerous sneaker collaborations with the likes of Nike, adidas, New Balance and Puma. Their attention to detail and knowledge of the culture help create some of the most beautiful and informed releases on the scene.

www.crookedtongues.com

CROOKED TONGUES

ADIDAS ADICOLOR BK3

Created as a tribute to the most basic form of customization, the lace switch, Crooked Tongues decided to take things one step further. This classic adidas silhouette features a choice of six sets of laces and six removable tongues in different colours: red, yellow, black, white, purple and green. Third in the adicolor black series (hence the BK3), the various colour combinations allow the whole look of the shoe to change against the solid, neutral black background. As Crooked Tongues put it: 'Co-ordination is a problem, and we're faintly obsessive about colour matching, because nothing screams NO EFFORT more than a mismatch between sneakers and garments. Consider this our donation to the shoe world – a trainer that's adaptable to your entire wardrobe.' See the rest of the adidas adicolor project on pages 108–113.

Thrash-metal black meets b-boy-style self-expression – the colours of this tactile and collectable sneaker also reflect the general look of the Crooked Tongues website, even down to the speckled midsole that incorporates minuscule splashes of the entire colour palette.

NEW BALANCE CONFEDERATION OF VILLAINY

Crooked Tongues' third collaboration with New Balance saw a collection of four different sneakers, each themed after a particular historical villain. Named the Confederation of Villainy, the pack consisted of an NB 1500 (themed on the pirate Blackbeard), an NB 577 (themed on Chinese outlaw Song Jiang , aka Black Sword), an NB 575 (themed around crook of the Old West Black Bart) and an NB 991 (themed on Bedfordshire highwayman Black Tom).

Bored with the generic boxes stacked in their closets, Crooked Tongues worked with tattoo artist BJ Betts to produce themed premium packaging featuring Betts's obsessively detailed art.

All four shoes in the edition feature a white metal top eyelet and unique Confederation of Villainy tongue label.

Retailing at £150 and available only through the Crooked Tongues online store, only 99 pairs of each colourway were made.

BLACK TOM
The NB 991 pays homage to the mysterious highwayman, and one-time scourge of Bedfordshire, Black Tom. The choice of the 991, considered the staple New Balance shoe worldwide, for this release was a refreshing departure from the usual collaboration fodder. New Balance kindly allowed Crooked Tongues to incorporate a custom sole on this model – the Abzorb midsole now blends with the colours of its attached upper, while the outsole incorporates a neon green. The panel on the heel was also altered to read 991 instead of UK.

BLACK SWORD
Chinese outlaw Song Jiang (aka Black Sword) was the reference for this New Balance 577.

BLACK BART
Using a super-durable gum outsole, this New Balance 575 is themed after Black Bart, the gentleman crook of the Old West.

BLACK BEARD
This New Balance 1500 uses a mix of black, white and grey, with a burst of fluorescent red to reflect the villain after whom the shoe was themed: Blackbeard, the ruthless pirate who allegedly placed lit matches in his beard. Given the dark subject matter, a black midsole was also incorporated.

PUMA CROOKED CLYDE

Crooked Tongues teamed up with Puma in 2006 to launch the CT (Crooked Tongues) Clyde, a trilogy of releases that took inspiration from the early days of hip-hop and b-boy style. 'We were trying to cater to the heads still hunting the rust-coloured pair from a misspent youth as well as some kid fiending for something bright, wearable and different from the rest', explains Crooked Tongues.

To coincide with the project, and as part of the Crooked Tongues website's Clyde retrospective, users were given the opportunity to design and submit their ideas for the third CT Clyde. Out of more than 700 online entries, Crooked Tongues member albellisimo's yellow and orange creation was chosen.

Each colourway was limited to just 300 pairs worldwide and dropped exclusively to Crooked Tongues online store (with matching T-shirt and keyring) before becoming available at select retailers.

 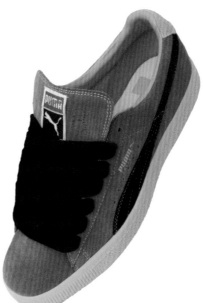 

CT CLYDE TIMELINE
AS SHOWN HERE, THE DEVELOPMENT OF THE CT CLYDES WAS DOCUMENTED AT EACH POINT OF THE DESIGN PROCESS VIA THE CROOKED TONGUES WEBSITE.

First Round Samples
March 2006

CROOKED TONGUES' COMMENTS:
Contrast stitching does not work right across the board. On the green shoe, the stitching is lighter than the suede and this creates nice holes – gaps, almost, between each stitch. But on the grey shoe, the stitching is darker, which creates the illusion of an unbroken line – not as nice.

CROOKED TONGUES' CHANGES:
CT Clyde 1
1. Please change the Darkest Spruce colour to black.
2. Please use new foot bed artwork.

CT Clyde 2
1. Please change the Chilli Pepper colour to a deeper burgundy, less red colour. Ref. PMS 188.
2. Please change the Dawn Blue (darker grey) colour to a darker shade. Ref. PMS 405.
3. Please can we change the Neutral Grey to a slightly darker shade (more dirt-resistant). Ref. PMS 421.
4. Can we please lose the red stitching and replace it with Neutral Grey stitching.
5. Please use new foot bed artwork.

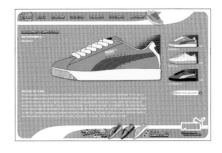

The insole of the Crooked Clyde pays homage to the electronic design and iconic typography of the early 1980s. 'Our shoes pay tribute to a time when invention and individuality were the done thing.'

The winning design of the Crooked Puma Clyde competition, as seen on the Crooked Tongues website. Users were able to design and submit their own colourway idea using an online template and colour palette. All uploaded entries were displayed in the online gallery.

Second Round Samples
June 2006

Final Approval
September 2006

CROOKED TONGUES' COMMENTS:
CT Clyde 1
The base colour has become lighter, which is a definite no-no. The print definition is different to the first sample; we like the 'Electro' design on the foot bed, but the font is wrong. On the plus side, we're very happy with the edition of black. It works a lot better than the dark green before.

CT Clyde 2
The base colour should have been a darker grey, like the form stripe on the first sample. It isn't. It seems to have become lighter. The form stripe and co-ordinating details have taken an unwelcome and unexpected jump from grey to teal! The red on the midsole was meant to be darker, but it's a lot lighter instead. As with the greens, the foot bed font issue is intact. However, it's not all bad... we're happy that the stitching isn't red anymore.

CROOKED TONGUES' COMMENTS:
After another sample of the CT Clyde 2 that was too washed out, the designs are finally approved.

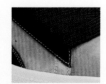

www.bjbetts.com

CUBANBEE

Renowned tattoo artist and Crooked Tongues crewmember BJ Betts (aka Cubanbee) collaborated with Puma for this retro of the 1986 running shoe the RS-100. Three colours make up the trilogy – green, brown and orange – and the shoes also feature three themed heel prints depicting old tattoo favourites – Mom (orange), Dad (blue) and the Sacred Heart (green), which blend ink with stitching to reflect the skin-art theme of this release.

Tattoo artist Betts is particularly famed for his unique writing styles, which make an appearance on the insole. The release also features a skin-colour midsole.

SCOTT BOURNE

Puma and US skater Scott Bourne teamed up for the introduction of the Puma S, a clean and classic skate silhouette that takes its inspiration from the Puma Suede and Clyde. 'We rode Puma Suedes and Clydes long before any skate shoe. You couldn't get Vans in North Carolina at the time so we rode whatever worked best on our boards.'

A well-established professional skater and creative force in the writing community, Bourne customized the shoe with his words and drawings. One of his poems is featured on the lining; he sketched the 'Follow No One' piece on the tongue label and crafted the heelpiece with his long-time hourglass logo.

Available in black, team regal red or steel grey, the shoe also comes with customized tissue paper featuring Bourne's drawings. A limited run of 100 pairs also contained a signed photo from Bourne.

Bourne first used his hourglass logo on a Consolidated skateboard project nearly ten years ago. 'At that time it had no wings,' says Bourne. 'It simply meant memento mori, which is Latin for "remember you must die". To me it was about chasing time, making every moment count.' The wings were added to represent the Latin tempus fugit, which translates literally as "time flies". The poem (featured on the inside of the shoe) was written long before the Puma collaboration arose, as Bourne explains. 'It was basically about being poor and going to school in worn-out shoes. I compared that scenario to having tattoos; I have simply grown out of something I am still forced to wear.'

MOTUG

This shoe from JB Classics was produced, designed and developed in conjunction with MÖTUG (Monsters Of The Unda-Ground) as the world's largest artist footwear collaboration. The ten artists involved were Futura 2000, NYC Lase, Doze Green, Ghost, Shepard Fairey (Obey), Ewok, Toofly, CES, TKID 170 and Dizmology. The shoes, a JB Country Club Mid model, were limited to just 24 pairs (only seven of which were actually made available to the public) and were released at the Showroom NYC Gallery in New York at US$1500 a pair.

www.damovement.org

NYC LASE/DAMOVEMENT

The JB Classics Peddler model was used to create this collaboration with artist NYC Lase and his DaMovement project, which aims to raise awareness and funds for various charitable causes. In this case the fundraising was for the Invisible Children and Paradox's project, Restoration (a charity for eating disorders).

    Limited to 50 pairs worldwide, and dubbed DaZebras, the shoes include a patent toe box, a quilted leather side panel, a clear sole and a zebra-hair heel. The tongue tag also includes a Love Is A Battlefield patch.

www.thequietlife.com

THE QUIET LIFE

The Quiet Life is a small art, design and clothing project run by designer, photographer and Lakai art director Andy Mueller. In 2007, the Lakai Limited-editions programme teamed up with The Quiet Life to produce this five-shoe collaboration. 'We'd been hinting for months about doing a shoe with Lakai,' says Mueller. 'When they first asked us we were expecting to do one shoe, so when it turned into five we couldn't believe it.'

The inspiration for the series comes from Mueller's graphics, with each release tying in to a different theme or graphic from The Quiet Life. Only limited releases of each style were made available.

The first shoe in the series, the Belmont, is based on The Quiet Life Camera Club – an online photo gallery featuring photographers from around the world. The insoles of the shoes feature a selection of images from the gallery.

The Telford uses text and imagery based on The Quiet Life Army, the online community of The Quiet Life. As Mueller explains, 'We're trying to be more than just a brand; we're trying to do things as a community.'

The visual for the MJ Select came from one of Mueller's graphics called Paint Swoosh. 'It's as if a paintbrush could leave slogans and phrases instead of just colours. I like the idea of painting the world with words.'

The fourth shoe in the series, the Manchester, is derived from another of Mueller's graphics called Half Of A Secret Handshake. The graphic was blended with the Lakai logo, turning it into a fist holding the Lakai icon.

The idea for the Caracas, a running shoe, was taken from a solo show Mueller had in Paris called 'All Day All Night'. The graphic for the show used two intersecting paintbrush strokes to convey the idea that Mueller was always working on more than one project at a time. 'I feel like I'm always working on things, always running around doing a million projects at once. So it made complete sense to me to put this graphic and text on a running shoe.'

www.kidrobot.com

KIDROBOT

Since its birth in the late 1990s, the vinyl toy movement exploded into the consciousness of artists and designers worldwide. Founded in 2002 by designer Paul Budnitz, Kidrobot is the world-famous creator and retailer of limited-edition art toys and apparel, operating three store/gallery spaces in New York, San Francisco and Los Angeles. Many of Kidrobot's toys and clothing feature collaborations with graffiti artists, graphic designers, illustrators and musicians, including the likes of Frank Kozik, Tilt and Dalek.

Shuttlemax is a limited-edition vinyl space shuttle based on the Nike Air Max 95. Produced in collaboration with art director and designer Bill McMullen, just 300 lime, 200 red and 100 yellow editions were produced. www.billmcmullen.com

LACOSTE

In 2007 Kidrobot teamed up with Lacoste to launch a collection of three sneakers. Paul Budnitz and Chad Philips from Kidrobot chose three patterns that matched their toy lines to use on the collection. For the Missouri 85, Kidrobot opted to use their monochrome bones pattern. The Revan 3 features an eyeball pattern, while the Revan 2 uses the Kidrobot head logo. The insole of each sneaker is also printed with the Kidrobot head logo and the shoes feature 3M reflective highlights. Each of the three styles was produced in a limited edition of 500 pairs worldwide and each pair comes with its own PEECOL toy (customized to match its respective sneaker) created by eBoy and Kidrobot.

JB CLASSICS

The blue JB Getlo sneaker marked the beginning of a series of footwear developed by JB Classics Lab in conjunction with Kidrobot and the artist Tilt. Made from nubuck leather, the shoe features the Tilt bubble design and a gold interior. The shoe was distributed through Kidrobot in 2006.

The second collaboration used an all-black JB Peddler model and again featured Tilt's colourful artwork. The shoe also features Kidrobot lace locks, and material combinations and accent colouring by JB Classics designer Mdot. Limited to 240 pairs globally, the shoe was distributed through Kidrobot in 2007, along with a matching crew neck hoodie. As with all JB Classics releases, both shoes were hand-numbered and packaged with an official certificate of ownership.

NIKE

The Nike Air Max 1 is probably Kidrobot's most famous foray into the world of sneakers. Produced in 2005 as a collaboration between Kidrobot, Nike and Barneys (the New York department store), both styles of the shoe feature gum rubber soles and a heat-embossed Kidrobot logo on the heel. Each pair comes in a custom gold and pink drawer-style collector's box and includes a special limited-edition Kidrobot keychain and one of five blind-chase sock liners created by artists Gary Baseman, Dalek, David Horvath, Huck Gee and Frank Kozik. Just 250 pairs of the black edition were produced worldwide – with the pink hyperstrike edition (which was not actually for sale) limited to 24 pairs.

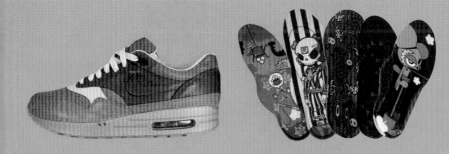

NIKE HTM AIR WOVEN RAINBOW

These shoes were created as part of the Nike HTM project and are made from multi-coloured woven material. Released in 2002, a number of colourways were produced, ranging from classic greyscale to the multi-coloured version shown here. Just 1500 pairs of each colourway were released.

NIKE HTM AIR WOVEN BOOT

Part of the HTM project, these sneakers are also made from woven material. The shoes were individually numbered and limited to 1500 pairs worldwide. Released in 2002, the shoe was available in black, brown and khaki.

www.fragment.jp

HIROSHI FUJIWARA

Japanese artist, designer and musician Hiroshi Fujiwara is a pioneer in collaboration. He has worked with the likes of Converse, Nike, Burton and Levi's, while also developing his own brands Goodenough and Head Porter. His sneaker work can also be more than just colourway application, developing new shoe design concepts and hybrids like the Nike Air Footscape Woven and the Air Woven Boot.

Fujiwara was also a founding member of web magazine *honeyee.com*, where he writes a blog. His artwork can be viewed at www.fragment.jp.

NIKE AIR FOOTSCAPE WOVEN

Inspired by the 1995 Nike Air Footscape, the Air Footscape Woven uses an innovative woven design for its upper. The version shown here is made from patent leather and was part of Fujiwara's Polka Dot Pack, a tier zero release which also included a Dunk Low and an Air Force 1.

NIKE AIR FOOTSCAPE WOVEN CHUKKA

This shoe combines the sole unit from the Air Footscape and the upper from the HTM Air Woven Boot, using a suede-like woven material. Released in 2006, they were available in brown (with a blue outsole), sail (with a yellow outsole) and black.

CONVERSE CHUCK TAYLOR ALL STAR

In 2007, Fujiwara joined forces with Converse to produce these black Chuck Taylor All Star shoes. The red low top version was produced for Converse (PRODUCT) RED collection which helps fight AIDS in Africa. All versions of the shoe feature Fujiwara's Fragment logo on the heel.

www.graphiknonsense.com

GRAPHIKNONSENSE

Graphiknonsense is the work of London-based Mark Ward. A freelance graphic artist, Ward has created images in his distinct style for brands such as Nike, Medicom and Stussy. Some of his best-known work has been for London sneaker boutique Foot Patrol, working on both sneaker collaborations and graphic design for the store. Ward describes himself as 'a washed-up skateboarder with a dodgy knee, who concentrates more on the graphics than the tricks these days.'

FOOT PATROL

As well as producing logos and artwork for London sneaker boutique Foot Patrol, Ward also worked on the design of this Nike Air Epic. The colour inspiration was military, with undertones of London, and the shoe features a graphic of a taxi, one of London's most iconic images, on the tongue. The box features a London-style road sign on the inside of the reversible box lid. Designed by Mark Ward, Steve Brydon, Michael Kopelman and Fraser Cooke.

NEW BALANCE SUPER TEAM 33

To create its highest-quality sneakers, New Balance created a special production line in their premier US factory, Skowhegan, Maine (a district famous for its shoe manufacturing). Super Team 33 – so-named because of the total number of members in the team – is made up of 28 highly experienced workers and five highly skilled craftsmen. In his ongoing post as design consultant for New Balance, Ward created the third (European) series in the Super Team 33 project. Dubbed the Fanzine series, this limited-edition NB 1400 release was inspired by homemade publications. The three colourways – red, blue and white – are a homage to popular fanzine paper stocks, and the punch perforations in the vamp and midsole symbolize the heavily inked dots that old typewriters would leave when typing on to fanzine paper. In direct contrast to the graphic subject matter of the series, the sneakers feature a combination of premium full-grain leathers and intricate printed materials. The lining says 'Do It Yourself' in several languages to reflect the worldwide nature of this release. Additional design by Craig Ford.

www.jeremyville.com

JEREMYVILLE

Dividing his time between studios in Sydney and New York, prolific artist, toy designer and animator Jeremyville has collaborated with many clients including Kidrobot, Coca-Cola, MTV and adidas (creating a custom sneaker design for the Australian leg of the adicolor world tour). Jeremyville also collects rare toys, clothing and sneakers.

In 2007 Jeremyville was invited to take part in the Converse 1HUND(RED) Artists programme, creating a design for a pair of Chuck Taylor high-tops. As Jeremyville explains, 'I initially painted a blank shoe that was sent to me (shown right), then I sent it back, and the art directors at Converse adapted the design to take into account production issues.' The finished version of the shoes (shown left) were released in 2008.

Jeremyville also worked closely with Converse and designer Damion Silver to create this one-off pair of Chuck Taylor high-tops. Silver first painted on the shoes in New York, then sent them to Jeremyville in Sydney to add his artwork.

www.dpmhi.com

JEAN-MICHEL BASQUIAT

First making their appearance in Reebok's I Am What I Am campaign, these Reebok Basquiat Reeboppers were designed by maharishi in conjunction with the Jean-Michel Basquiat estate, who had signed a multi-year contract with Reebok in 2005.

The shoes include a custom tag on the tongue, embroidered Basquiat artwork on the side of the shoe and a clear sole, through which you can see artwork by Basquiat.

Initially launched in 2005 at a Basquiat retrospective at the Museum of Contemporary Art in Los Angeles, a few pieces were also pre-launched at the DPMHI and maharishi stores in London. Only 500 pairs of each of the three colourways were produced.

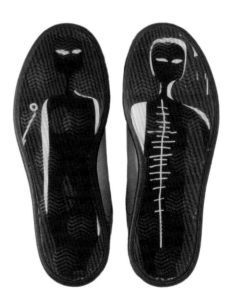

www.dalekart.com

DALEK

New York-based artist James Marshall is better known as Dalek, the pseudonym he used during his days as a graffiti writer. A self-taught painter (who once worked as an assistant to Japanese artist Takashi Murakami), Dalek has built an increasingly sophisticated body of work around the cartoon figure he calls Space Monkey. The character was born out of graffiti, but quickly transcended the genre into paintings, toys, prints – and now sneakers.

This collaboration with Dekline features Dalek's laser-etched artwork, allowing for minute detail in the design. The shoes use a combination of premium leathers and synthetics. Released in 2007, each pair comes with a numbered authenticity slip.

www.futura2000.com

FUTURA 2000

Probably the most famous graffiti artist on the planet, Futura 2000 (his name inspired by a combination of Stanley Kubrick's film *2001: A Space Odyssey* and the Futura typeface) was born in Brooklyn in 1955 as Lenny McGurr. Known for his highly skilled, uniquely abstract and futuristic style, Futura's graffiti was more about shape and textural pattern than lettering. He was a pioneer in transferring graffiti from the street to art galleries, and famously produced record sleeve artwork for punk band The Clash.

Futura's involvement in the music industry was revived in the 1990s (with the help of James Lavelle) when he produced artwork (alongside designer Ben Drury) for several of Lavelle's Mo' Wax releases – a collaboration that later defined the imagery of Lavelle's UNKLE project.

Much of Futura's work has been channelled towards the production of collectable toys and his involvement in the clothing industry. In the 1990s he started the Project Dragon line, as well as setting up New York's Recon store (with fellow graffiti legend Stash), and he has also collaborated with the likes of Nike, Phillie Blunt and Zoo York. He currently runs the Futura Laboratories clothing line.

NIKE DUNK HIGH PRO SB FLOM (FOR LOVE OR MONEY)
Only 24 pairs of these sneakers were ever made, with just three pairs going to the public as part of a raffle in Hong Kong. Each pair is made up of images of various currencies (meaning no one shoe is the same), with an embroidered FL logo on the heel. Released in 2005.

NIKE ZOOM AIR FC iD
In 2005, Nike and Futura collaborated to commemorate Lance Armstrong's seventh, and last, Tour de France. The Flance sneaker features a series of symbols and icons designed by Futura; the symbols were also reproduced on Armstrong's Tour de France time trial bike. As well as Nike's swoosh, the sneaker features the Lance L logo and the Futura Laboratories FL logo. As part of the 10/2 clothing line (commemorating the date when Armstrong was diagnosed with testicular cancer), 500 pairs of the sneakers were released to the public.

NIKE FREE TRAIL
Released in 2005.

NIKE PAUL RODRIGUEZ ZOOM AIR ELITE
Released in 2006, this shoe features patent leather and a clear swoosh.

www.methamphibian.com   www.royalefam.com

SKULLS OF SAIGON

It would be hard to produce a book about sneakers and art without mentioning customizers SBTG and Methamphibian. Both artists have rapidly made names for themselves as highly talented and prolific sneaker customizers, to the extent where they have collaborated with major brands on their own sneaker designs. The two became close friends after performing live customizations at a 'Sneaker Pimps' show (see pages 192–195), and have recently started to work together under the collective name Skulls Of Saigon.

METHAMPHIBIAN

Los Angeles-based Methamphibian is an ongoing project established in 2001 by Peter Kim, which encompasses art, design, illustration and graphic design. Methamphibian's design philosophy is based on DIY aesthetics and principles, making sneaker customization an obvious avenue for his talents. As with SBTG, Methamphibian's customization skills soon attracted the interest of a major sneaker brand, and the resulting collaboration with DC Shoes has so far produced two separate releases.

DC SHOES ARTIST PROJECTS™
Methamphibian has teamed up with DC Shoes to produce two separate releases; shown here is the first of these collaborations, produced in 2006. It features canvas and suede uppers accented with Methamphibian's custom-screened four-panel artwork. See pages 90 and 91 for information on the rest of the DC Shoes Artist Projects™ series.

SKULLS OF SAIGON

In 2007 SBTG and Methamphibian decided to unite their sneaker-customizing talents under the name Skulls of Saigon. Inspired by their shared love of 1980s thrash metal bands (the likes of Slayer, Sepultura, Pantera and Metallica), Skulls Of Saigon was created to provide a tongue-in-cheek side to the monotone and more serious custom designs the pair usually produce. This collaborative work still features some of the darker elements of Methamphibian's work, as well as SBTG's trademark pattern work, but together it creates a more energetic mix of colour and imagery.

SBTG

SBTG (a contraction of Sabotage) is Singaporean designer Mark Ong. What initially started as a hobby for Ong quickly turned into a full-time business after he won a custom competition on sneaker community website niketalk.com. Originally known for customizing (or sabotaging) only Nike shoes, it wasn't long before SBTG collaborated with Nike on a legitimate sneaker release, and in 2006 the (Asia exclusive) Nike Dunk Low Premium SB SBTG was released. Ong is also responsible for the clothing label Royalefam, an apparel range highly influenced by urban and war aesthetics.

NIKE DUNK LOW PREMIUM SB

Released in 2006 as an exclusive for the Asian market, the SBTG collaboration with Nike has the look and feel of a custom shoe; it even includes one of SBTG's trademark custom features, the lace cover. In 2007, a special friends-and-family version of the shoe was released (shown here), this time to a worldwide audience. This re-release featured the inclusion of new laces, a special lace lock and a specially designed slide box.

Hong Kong-based lifestyle brand CLOT was established in 2003 by Edison Chen, Kevin Poon and Billy Ip. It specializes in almost everything involved in youth culture and was started as a creative outlet and showcase for fashion, music, design and entertainment.

The Kiss Of Death Nike Air Max 1 was CLOT's first sneaker collaboration. It was inspired by the pressure point (known as Kiss of Death) that is located at the centre of the foot; supposedly the most lethal pressure point in the human body. The original concept came from Hong Kong graffiti artist MC Yan, with the team at CLOT providing the additional design details.

Released to purely Tier Zero accounts, the shoes were stocked in only a handful of stores around the world. The Hong Kong edition came with a special-edition box and manual, resembling an ancient Chinese book.

www.clotinc.com

CLOT/ACU

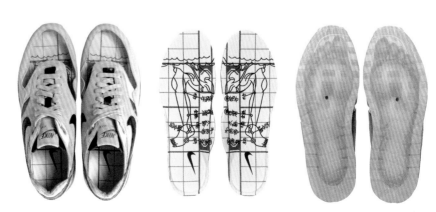

NIKE AIR MAX 1

This Nike Air Max 1 was made to commemorate the collaboration between Edison Chen and Kanye West in the Hong Kong leg of West's Touch the Sky Tour – where Chen performed the opening act. The shoe features a laser-engraved CLOT logo on the heel, and the word 'clot' on the mudguard. There are only four pairs of these in existence, two going to CLOT and two to Kanye West.

NIKE RASTA PACK

CLOT, in conjunction with their sneaker boutique ACU, also designed this Rasta pack. The pack consisted of a Nike Footscape Woven and a Nike Dunkesto, both of which used hemp as the main material. First issued as a hyperstrike release to commemorate the opening of ACU in Shanghai, the shoes were later produced as a quickstrike release and could be found in most major cities. The shoes released at the ACU store, however, included a limited-edition wooden shoebox.

NECKFACE

California-based Neckface is a skateboarder and artist whose graffiti has assaulted urban landscapes around the world. Best known for his uniquely scratchy and violent drawing style, Neckface made his name on the streets of San Francisco and later New York, stickering and scrawling his art on to various buildings and street signs.

For this collaboration with Vans in 2007, Neckface created individual art pieces for the DD-66, AV Era, TNT 2, and Sk8-Hi models, along with matching T-shirts and a hat.

www.howlingprint.com

DENNIS MCNETT

New York-based Dennis McNett is a skateboarder and artist known for his bold linocut print work. In 2008, McNett collaborated with the limited-edition line Vans Syndicate on this pack of four sneakers, comprising a Sk8 Low, a Rowley Shambles, a Slip-On and a No School Mid. 'I had originally done some skateboard designs for the company Antihero and was going to do a shoe for one of their riders. That fell through but I was then asked to do shoes for the Vans skate team. They were really open and supportive of whatever I wanted to do. I asked what they thought the riders would want and tried to create images for them.' A series of T-shirts was also created for the release.

www.stapledesign.com

STAPLE DESIGN

New York-based Staple Design is a prolific independent visual communications agency – as much a cultural barometer as a business. The founder and owner of the brand, which includes Staple Clothing and Staple's New York store, Reed Space, is Jeff Ng (aka Jeff Staple). Multi-talented Staple is a graphic, web and clothing designer, artist, DJ, writer, entrepreneur and world-renowned blogger. 'I know how long I've been into shoes and it started at an extremely young age,' says Staple. 'But it's hard to explain why. I think since I was young, shoes were sort of a status symbol. They showed how fly you were... or how stylish you were.'

Staple has worked with numerous brands, including New Balance, Levi's, Puma, Timberland, Uniqlo, Apple and Sony PlayStation, to name but a few, and has enjoyed repeated collaboration success with Nike. Sneaker fans probably best know Staple for his role in the creation of the New York Dunk, which caused mass hysteria on its release.

GRAVIS BLACK BOX EDITION
Staple produced these three sneakers (the Gravis Lodown, Dune and Royale) in 2007 for Gravis's exclusive Black Box collection. 'When snow falls in New York, it is beautiful on the first day. Then, as the days progress, it slowly turns into this slushy, muddy pile of nastiness. This really reminds me of the old New York, so I wanted to develop an icon that represented both city and snow.' Staple developed a specific colour palette that drew inspiration from this idea, resulting in a series of colours named Fresh Powder, Wet Cement and Parking Lot. The colours were then applied to the various shoes and bags in this very limited edition. The Royale (as it was the low cut) represented the Fresh Powder, the Lodown (because it was the mid cut) represented the Wet Cement, and the high cut Dune represented the Parking Lot.

NIKE DUNK LOW SB (PIGEON)

Produced in 2005 as part of the 'White Dunk' exhibition (see page 200–207), this shoe is highly regarded as one of the most coveted sneakers of all time. The shoe was themed on the city of New York – with the design being based on a pigeon. Only 150 pairs of this sneaker were produced, causing a near-riot when they were released to the public through Staple's Reed Space store.

NIKE NORDIC PACK

Produced in 2006, this pack of a Nike AF1 Low, a Dunk Low and an Air Stab were based on three previous winter Olympic games – at Sapporo, Lillehammer and Salt Lake City. Merino wool and leather inlays were used throughout the design, with each sock liner featuring a map of each of the Olympic cities.

NIKE AIR FORCE 1 (MY FIRST LOVE)

This was a customized Nike AF1 produced in 2003 for the first ever 'Sneaker Pimps' exhibition (see page 192–195). The design was a combination of Staple's two first loves: sneakers and Linn Minmei from the Japanese animation *Robotech*.

NIKE DUNK LOW NRF EDITION

NRF stands for the Nike Recess Federation, a basketball league run for Nike under the Staple Design umbrella. NRF is a highly exclusive group of New York's most influential creatives playing organized basketball each week, with the finals at Madison Square Garden. This sneaker was the trophy for the winning team. Twelve pairs were produced.

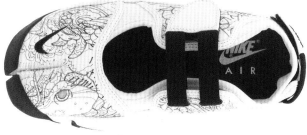

NIKE TATTOO SERIES
Created in 2004, this was the first mass-produced project involving Nike's laser technology and uses art based on traditional Japanese tattoo techniques. Staple produced two shoes for the project, the Nike Original Cortez and the Air Rift + (sample version shown here). The Air Rift + was created to appeal to the female sneaker market.

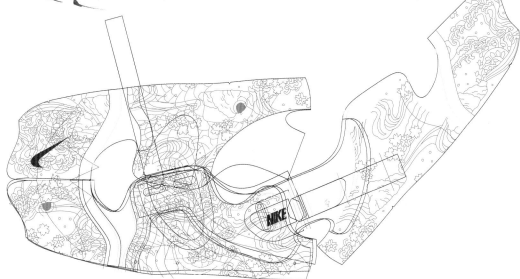

NIKE NAVIGATION PACK
Staple and Nike created this pack (featuring a Nike Air Burst, Air Max 90 and Shox NZ) especially for the sneaker hunter who is willing to cross air, land and sea to find their holy grail. 'Sneakerheads are the navigators of our time,' says Staple. The Air Burst is dedicated to the sea and is laser-etched with graphics of water currents that flow around the country of Japan. The Air Max 90 is dedicated to the land and has a block-by-block map of Lower Manhattan lasered onto the upper. The Shox NZ model is dedicated to the air and features jet-stream patterns from around the UK.

ROBERT WILLIAMS

The controversial painter Robert Williams (shown opposite, below left) is probably best known for his depiction of robot to human rape and brutality on the album cover of *Appetite For Destruction* by Guns N' Roses (controversy later forced Geffen Records to move the artwork to the inside cover).

The founder of *Juxtapoz Art & Culture Magazine*, Williams began his career as a part of the innovative and groundbreaking Zap Collective, alongside underground cartoonist revolutionaries like Robert Crumb, and his art can be described as a mix of Californian hot rod culture, film noir and psychedelic imagery.

In 2007, Williams's artwork featured on this series of shoes from Vans Vault. Launched in 2003, the Vans Vault line was created to give designers the ability to experiment with fabrics and prints, while maintaining Vans' classic design. Williams's series includes two Slip-On Lx, a Sk8 Hi and a Chukka 69 Lx.

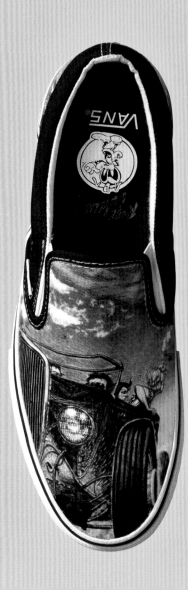

MARK GONZALES

Mark Gonzales (aka The Gonz) is an artist and professional skateboarder, best known as a pioneer of street skateboarding. Originally sponsored by skateboarding company Vision, Gonzales founded Blind skateboards in 1989 (the name was an intentional slight to Vision). He is currently sponsored by a host of companies, including adidas and Krooked Skateboarding (a company he also runs).

When adidas originally approached Gonzales to design a signature skateboarding shoe, he wanted it to be made of wood, 'so you have wood on the board and wood inside your shoe. It would be more natural; you could almost feel the soul of the tree'. Unfortunately, the project was never produced.

Known for his canvas paintings and customized priest characters, Gonzales has also established a parallel career as an artist, having shown at various galleries worldwide. Collectors of his work allegedly include Donald Trump and Sean Combs (P. Diddy). Gonzales is also a published author and poet, and designs the Japanese clothing line Gonzo Cuntry.

Shown here are the Gonzales' adidas Superskate Vulcanized Slip-On and High, and Stan Smith Skate (main picture).

Gonzales teamed up with adidas in 2007 to promote Skate, a skateboarding computer game from Electronic Arts. The Mark Gonzales High Score Superstar Skate was limited to 500 pieces, and getting your hands on a pair was only possible (via the adidas website) after unlocking secret codes within the game. Professional skateboarder Dennis Busenitz also produced a sneaker (the High Score Gazelle Skate) as part of the project.

These adidas Stan Smith Skate's were hand painted by Gonzales during a visit to London in 2007. Gonzales customized the shoes while painting 1000 of his Megga America Communion Priest characters for an exhibition at the DPMHI gallery.

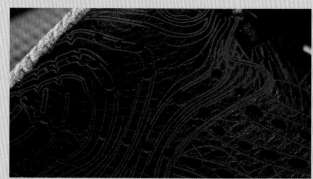

www.artthequestion.com

TOM LUEDECKE

In 1997, Nike released the original Air Talaria sneaker to wide acclaim throughout the running community. The Air Talaria has always been a classic running shoe, loved for both its comfort and unusual use of vibrant colours.

In 2006, German-born Nike designer Tom Luedecke (an artist in his own right) and the Innovation Kitchen (Nike's technological development centre) took this iconic running silhouette and fused it with design, technology and street style to create the Talaria Chukka.

The top has been laser-etched with a design by Luedecke that mimics the anatomical structure of the foot, complete with bones, nerves, blood vessels, tendons, muscles and veins. A similar mapping of the foot's structure is displayed on the outsole, just beneath the cover of clear rubber. The Talaria Chukka also offers a supremely well-crafted fit, with minimal foam padding on the inside of the shoe.

This Tier Zero release was available in two colourways, the first using mainly black and dark brown, with the second adding neon yellow and pink highlights for a more traditional Talaria appearance. Photography by Ryan Unruh.

This white version of the shoe is a handcrafted sample created by Luedecke.

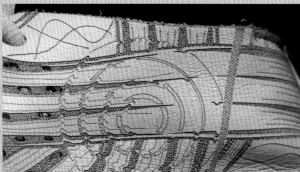

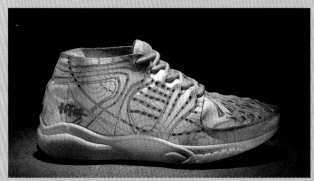

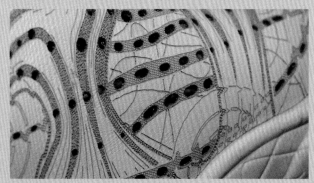

DAVE KINSEY

World-renowned street and fine artist Dave Kinsey is most famous for his haunting portraits of urban characters. Based in Los Angeles, Kinsey works with a range of media, including wood, canvas, paint, found materials, pen and ink – and sneakers. He also founded creative design agency (and gallery) Blk/Mrkt, working with clients such as Absolut, adidas, Royal Elastics, Heineken, DC Shoes and Nissan.

In 2006, Kinsey, with fellow artist Evan Hecox (see opposite), teamed up with adidas to create a limited-edition sneaker (and accompanying advertising campaign) for the launch of adidas Originals Skateboarding. Kinsey produced this Superstar Skate inspired by the city of San Diego, with his graffiti-based graphics laser-etched on to a limited run of 1000 sneakers.

www.evanhecox.com

EVAN HECOX

Evan Hecox is a Colorado-based illustrator and skateboarder known for his unique style and subtle depictions of urban environments. As well as producing numerous skateboard graphics and T-shirts for skateboarding brands Chocolate and Girl, Hecox has famously produced work for Carhartt clothing and has been a regular contributor to *Arkitip* magazine (see page 183).

For the launch of the adidas Originals Skateboarding line in 2006, Hecox (together with Dave Kinsey) created a limited-edition sneaker, along with an accompanying advertising campaign. Hecox's creation, a Stan Smith Skate, was beautifully screened with his artwork of the San Francisco cityscape and limited to 1000 pairs.

www.mikegiant.com

MIKE GIANT

Graffiti artist, tattooist, designer and illustrator, Mike Giant is a prolific
and versatile artist famed for his signature style, which mixes Mexican
folk art and Japanese illustration with religious symbolism. Amazingly,
Giant is colour-blind and nearsighted, part of the reason he mostly
works in high-contrast black and white. Born in New York and currently
based in Albuquerque, Giant initially studied architecture before
producing his first design work for Think skateboards. In recent years,
Giant has shown his artwork in galleries worldwide, as well as
designing for streetwear label Rebel8.

In 2007, Giant collaborated with adidas on this Superskate Low.
The sneakers were made from hemp material and featured Giant's
skull artwork and signature graffiti logo on the side.

www.dondiwhitefoundation.org

MICHAEL WHITE x DONDI WHITE

The late graffiti legend Dondi White (who died in 1998) was part of the 1970s New York graffiti scene when the city's Metropolitan Transit Authority eradicated graffiti writing from its trains. White (born Donald J. White) became one of a select group of street artists who began to work above ground and was at the heart of New York's art scene in the 1980s.

In 2007, Converse worked with the White family on this Pro Leather 76 shoe as the first of 100 for the Converse 1HUND(RED) Artists project supporting (PRODUCT) RED. Working closely with White's brother Michael, Converse produced a shoe featuring White's artwork on the insole, the outer and through the transparent outer sole.

(PRODUCT) RED is an economic initiative designed to deliver a sustainable flow of private sector money to the Global Fund to invest in African AIDS programs with an emphasis on the health of women and children. Since White's death, the Dondi White Foundation has been fundraising for AIDS charities, making this a perfect collaboration.

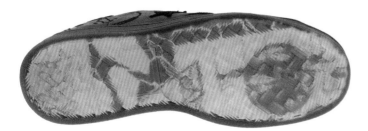

www.mistercartoon.com

MR. CARTOON

Earning his name through his drawing abilities and personality, Mr. Cartoon (aka Mark Machado) is one of the world's premier tattoo artists, having inked the likes of Nas, Eminem and Method Man. Famed for his intricate masterpieces, Cartoon uses a technique called fine line tattooing, which originated in US prisons where black ink was watered down to create shadows and depth, as coloured inks just weren't available.

As well as being a world-renowned tattoo artist, Mr. Cartoon was a founder of the Joker clothing brand and also finds the time to take part in various artistic collaborations. Finding his calling in hip-hop, Cartoon was originally introduced to art and design through a career in graffiti back in the 1980s. He has since worked on sneaker collaborations with both Nike and Vans, produced album cover artwork (most famously for Cypress Hill) and created backdrops for music promos – he even created graffiti backdrops for Rockstar's hip-hop themed game Grand Theft Auto: San Andreas.

The Mr. Cartoon Vans Syndicate Sk8-Hi pack from 2007 (below) featured embroidered artwork on industrial strength canvas. Available in khaki, indigo and green.

TAKA HAYASHI

Self-taught painter, illustrator and graphic designer Taka Hayashi was born in Japan in 1971 and moved to the US in 1981. He grew up in Santa Monica where the early 1980s skateboarding scene had a huge impact on his life. He began drawing at a very early age and spent most of his time either skating or experimenting with art.

In 2008, Hayashi designed this incredibly detailed series of shoes for the Vans signature skateboarding team – Geoff Rowley, Anthony Van Engelen, Dustin Dollin and Tony Trujillo. Each design is inspired by the relevant skateboarder's unique style. Using a variety of different techniques and materials, Hayashi's art is strikingly reproduced on the (Geoff Rowley) Rowley Shambles, the (Anthony Van Engelen) AV Sk8 Low, the (Dustin Dollin) DD-66 and the (Tony Trujillo) TNT III Slip-On.

A series of four T-shirts (the Sixty-Six, Sk8 Til Death, Eagle Talon and Gangstar Bunny) were also released to complement the sneakers.

Continuing the creative partnership, Vans and Hayashi created this Vans Chukka and Slip-On (below) in 2008 as part of the Vans Vault line.

www.wk.com

WIEDEN + KENNEDY

In 2007, Wieden + Kennedy, the world's largest private advertising agency, marked their 25th anniversary and 25-year-long agency relation with Nike by producing this set of six Dunk Trainer Lows. The concept is the result of a collaboration between Nike designers and W+K employees, and the shoes are a hybrid of the Nike Free Trail, the Air Trainer 1 and the Dunk.

The six different colourways represent the different W+K offices around the world; green for Portland, orange for Amsterdam, yellow for New York, red for Shanghai, white for Tokyo and blue for London. The upper of the shoe is made from dark grey denim, grey suede and grey leather, and the forefoot strap features the lettering XXV.

The quotes on the insoles read:

'Everything can be reduced to math or emotion. For Nike and Wieden & Kennedy, 1+1 = can you #*&%ing believe it? Quite a run and we've just begun!' Mark Parker

'This shoe sits empty while you think back on all the two of you have accomplished – all you have laid witness to – and yet this shoe can't help wondering how long before you stop the reminiscence, before you take new roads to new places. This shoe sits empty.' Dan Wieden

C-LAW

Chris Law (C-Law) began his obsession with sneakers in 1983, during the football terrace style heyday and hip-hop's global boom. In the late 1990s, while working at the seminal London street-wear store Bond International, Law met his future business partner, Russell Williamson.

Williamson had an idea for an online project (later named Spinemagazine.com) and was also keen to start a small design firm that could focus its work on more street-based projects – a vision that later came to pass under the name Unorthodox Styles.

As part of the early incarnation of the Spinemagazine website, a feature on the topic of sneaker culture generated sufficient positive feedback to incite the next key in-house project for the Unorthodox Styles team – Crooked Tongues, a sneaker related website named after the aesthetically displeasing phenomenon in which a shoe's tongue doesn't sit straight (see page 34).

After more than six years at Unorthodox Style/Crooked Tongues, Law was approached by adidas to create his own line of shoes. The brief was to create designs that would appeal to 'heads' without sacrificing commercial appeal. Part of that range is presented here.

As Law explains, 'I'm a graphic designer and typographer by trade, but a shoe enthusiast by nature, so this is more of a design collaboration rather than an artist collaboration. I wanted to keep the graphics to a minimum and the wearability to a maximum.'

From left to right, the models shown here are the adidas Metro Attitude, Forum Low, ZXZ ADV, Halfshell and the ZX600.

www.kenzominami.com

KENZO MINAMI

In 2005, New York-based artist and designer Kenzo Minami was featured in Reebok's I Am What I Am advertising campaign (along with Jay-Z, 50 Cent, Lucy Liu, Christina Ricci, Allen Iverson and Yao Ming). He was one of the few selected artists for the Artist Series and his campaign was run together with that of Jean-Michel Basquiat. As part of the campaign, Minami created his own model of the Reebok Instapump Fury, which was limited to only 500 pairs worldwide.

Describing his work as 'schizophrenia with precisely organized structure and self-contained tailor-made logic', Minami purposely ignored the ergonomic aspects of the shoe design. 'I think I did that to the point that I even ignored the aesthetical logic and function – it only made sense as an object. It was destined to clash with anything you would wear with it and everything around it.'

KEN LINK &
MICHAEL SPOLJARIC

This Nike Zoom LeBron III is the result of a creative partnership between Nike Basketball footwear design director Ken Link, Nike Basketball art director Michael Spoljaric and London-based design studio Non-Format. Spoljaric had commissioned Non-Format to work on the overall identity for the LeBron III campaign and wanted to create a version of the shoe featuring the studio's unique typographic style. The sneaker was initially created as a one-off for basketball legend LeBron James to wear during a 2006 All Star basketball game, but was eventually released to the public in limited numbers, with Link creating the additional white and grey colourway.

Link and Spoljaric also collaborated on this Nike Zoom LeBron IV when Link had the idea of featuring the LeBron Code (Nike's internal marketing strategy for LeBron James) on a shoe. Since the LeBron Code is not an external marketing campaign, Spoljaric wanted the design to be abstract, and so created a grafitti based textural pattern using the words from the code: family, fearless, passion, vision and winning. Two colourways were produced for this very limited released – a white, black and red version (released only in New York at the LeBron pop-up store in SoHo), and the blue and white All Star version shown left.

www.junwatanabe.jp

JUN WATANABE

Born in Japan in 1977, Jun Watanabe is a designer and art director who specializes in the fashion and music industries. For this collaboration Watanabe combined his hands motif (a recurring element of his work) with the Madfoot! brand to create the Madhands project.

Watanabe's drawings appear on the canvas of this Mad Base model and the choice of pink stitching and purple leather creates a shoe in tune with the streets of Tokyo.

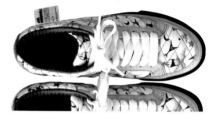

www.write-left.com

WRITE-LEFT

Based in Vancouver, Write-Left is a multi-disciplinary design studio encompassing the fields of graphic, interior and product design. Run by Kenta (who was born in Japan and raised in Canada), the studio's work is a fusion of the detailed aesthetics of Japan and the classic boldness of the US. Kenta is also one half of Brknhome, a T-shirt brand known for its bold graphic designs.

This 2007 collaboration with Etnies Plus (a numbered, limited-edition shoe series that uses unusual fabrics and hand-stitched construction) features two models, the Pablo and the Junior, and is accompanied by two co-branded T-shirts.

2001

2002

SHEPARD FAIREY

With DC's Swift model as its canvas, the Swift-Obey became the first Artist Projects™ shoe to be released. Fairey coupled his unique Obey character with a handpicked color scheme, and his artwork is also on the accompanying poster and shoe box.

KAWS

Street artist Kaws refined his Companion character to graphics that fit nicely on the sole, insole and uppers of DC's Gauge model.

THOMAS CAMPBELL

Using the same Swift model as Shepard Fairey, painter, illustrator, photographer and filmmaker Thomas Campbell contrasted the Swift-Obey with a more subdued shoe upper.

2003

ARKIGRAPH
DC joined with Arkitip Magazine and Even Hecox to create this Arkigraph shoe.

DAVE KINSEY
Artist and designer Dave Kinsey (who also conceptualized the DC logo) chose to enhance DC's Coda shoe as he liked its clean profile.

PHIL FROST
Self-taught artist Phil Frost developed this unique canvas high-top as well as creating the signature pattern and colourways. He also created the shoebox, hangtag art and helped developed a utility painter's bag that also bears his signature pattern.

www.dcshoes.com

DC SHOES ARTIST PROJECTS™

DC's Artist Projects™ was created in 2001 to recognize the creativity inherent in skateboarding. Working on the basis that skateboarders have always customized their shoes – either by drawing or painting on them, changing the laces or even cutting or modifying the shoe – the Artist Projects™ programme gives selected artists the opportunity to express themselves through the creation of special-edition DC shoes.

So far, artists who have taken part in the project include Shepard Fairey, KAWS, Dave Kinsey, Eric So, Phil Frost, Thomas Campbell, Arkitip/Evan Hecox, Andy Howell, Michael Leon, André, SSUR, Johanna Jackson, Methamphibian and Natas Kaupas. Shown here and overleaf is a timeline of each shoe produced in the project at the time this book went to press.

2004

ERIC SO
Named So Fun, this shoe was created by Hong Kong designer, illustrator and figure artist Eric So.

ANDY HOWELL
Famed skateboarder and artist Andy Howell re-worked DC's popular Alias model. The shoe features Howell's graffiti-inspired artwork and custom-illustrated insoles, and came in distinctive packaging coupled with a multi-page book designed by the artist.

2005

MICHAEL LEON
The Leon is a collaboration with artist and graphic designer Michael Leon.

ANDRÉ X ARKITIP
Grafitti artist André created 250 pairs of these unique hand-painted shoes in collaboration with *Arkitip* magazine. Each pair was also accompanied by a matching hipsack featuring an André print.

SSUR
This high-top by Russian-born artist Ruslan Karablin (aka SSUR) featured a specially designed sole and insole as well as a custom box which resembled a caviar tin. The black and silver colourway was limited to just 100 pairs and featured stingray material on the upper.

2006

JO JACKSON

Jo Jackson is a printer, animator, and sculptor based in Portland, Oregon. This Johanna shoe was specifically designed for womens sizing and fit.

MICHAEL LEON (RE-RUN)

ARKLEON

In collaboration with Arkitip magazine, the Arkleon draws inspiration from Michael Leon's 2005 shoe, The Leon. The Arkleon's simplistic design features a custom-designed mid top in water-resistant, breathable Wolverine® suede.

2007

METHAMPHIBIAN

DC teamed up with famed sneaker artist Methamphibian to create a custom-designed shoe along with a matching M65 styled jacket. Two additional versions of the shoe (limited to 48 pairs) were also produced for sneaker stores Brooklyn Projects (gum color) and In4mation (yellow).

NATAS KAUPAS

Considered one of the first professional street skaters, Natas Kaupas is also regarded as one of the industries most notable artists. His 'scribble' pattern artwork is integrated into the shoes' upper, insole and packaging.

SSUR

Inspired by his Russian heritage, SSUR's second collaboration with DC features printed floral leather and patent leather accents to give the appearance of blue paint baked onto white porcelain.

GRAVIS ART COLLECTIVE

Pushing artist collaborations to a whole new level, the 2005 Gravis Art Collective project began life as three original canvas artworks from urban artists Marok, Matt Sewell and Delta. Each artist created a 200 x 200cm canvas panel, which was then skillfully cut up to become part of a collection of Gravis Comet Mid shoes.

The artists not only integrated the fabric of their actual artwork but also decided their shoes' style direction, colourway and creative detailing. Gravis involved the artists at all stages of the product development, using the Collective as a testing ground for future artist collaborations. Only 36 shoes were made from each canvas. The project was showcased on a European tour before the shoes were released worldwide at selected outlets.

MATT SEWELL
www.mattsewell.co.uk

MAROK
www.marok.info

DELTA
www.deltainc.nl

ADIDAS SUPERSTAR 35ᵀᴴ ANNIVERSARY

In 2005, adidas celebrated the 35th anniversary of its most iconic shoe, the Superstar. The first Superstar went on sale in 1970 and, within a few years, was worn by more than 75 per cent of all NBA players. It quickly migrated from the basketball court to the street and evolved to become a cultural icon. Since then the shoe has become a design classic.

To commemorate the anniversary, adidas invited icons from the worlds of music, art and fashion to create five different series of unique Superstars (35 models in total) to honour a special place or time in the Superstar's history. The different styles created tell the shoe's story, from the humble beginnings of the 'shell toe' to its regular fixture in the worlds of fashion, music and film.

The five series – Consortium, Expression, Music, Cities and Anniversary – were made available through various distribution channels and covered a range of price levels. All 35 models were part of an integrated concept with a specially created Superstar 35 logo, each series featuring the logo in a distinguished colourway.

The Expression series holds particular interest, with leaders from the worlds of art, photography and graffiti contributing designs. Organizations such as Disney and The Andy Warhol Foundation, as well as the clothing company Project Playground and the artist Lee Quinones, created seven individually distinctive limited-edition Superstars.

MUSIC SERIES (UNRELEASED)
BEASTIE BOYS
This is the unreleased Beastie Boys Superstar, signed by MCA, Adrock & Mike D. These are probably the rarest of all the 35th Anniversary Superstars and were given only to the Beastie Boys themselves in recognition of their love of adidas over the years. Based on the New York editions, they feature embroidered Beastie Boys logos and the names of Mike D and Adrock on the heels.

EXPRESSION SERIES
CAPTAIN TSUBASA
In 1983, Youichi Takahashi sat down at home in Japan and drew the animated character Tsubasa Ozora, a boy destined to become the world's best football player. More than 25 years later, Captain Tsubasa has become a worldwide phenomenon and is almost single-handedly responsible for turning football into Japan's national obsession.

THE REST OF THE COLLECTION

CONSORTIUM SERIES

adi dassler	Footpatrol	Tate	Undefeated	Union	Neighbourhood	D-Mop

EXPRESSION SERIES
ANDY WARHOL
Appropriating images from popular culture, Andy Warhol is famed for his paintings of twentieth-century icons, from Campbell's soup cans to Marilyn Monroe. This Superstar celebrates his Athlete Series from the 1970s, featuring the basketball legend Kareem Abdul-Jabbar.

EXPRESSION SERIES
LEE QUINONES
Considered one of the most influential artists of the 1970s' New York subway graffiti movement, Lee Quinones' career has spanned more than three decades. Today, Lee's paintings are included in some of the most prestigious art collections around the globe.

MUSIC SERIES

| Run DMC | Ian Brown | Red Hot Chilli Peppers | Rocafella | Underworld | Bad Boy | Missy Elliot |

EXPRESSION SERIES
PROJECT PLAYGROUND
Justin Leonard founded Project Playground Clothing in 2000 as an independent company that embodies the playground culture of New York. Many of Project Playground's creative design concepts are derived from the proud community of which they are part – New York City basketball. Today more than ever, the close ties between basketball, art, music and fashion are being recognized and celebrated.

EXPRESSION SERIES
DISNEY
This shoe celebrates one of the most loved Disney characters, Goofy, who celebrated his 70th birthday in 2002 and started with a bit part in a Disney short.

CITY SERIES

Berlin	London	Paris	New York	Boston	Tokyo	Buenos Aires

EXPRESSION SERIES
ADICOLOR
adidas launched adicolor in 1984, making it one of the first customization projects executed on a global scale. The all-white shoes were delivered with a set of coloured weatherproof and quick-drying markers, allowing the wearers to create their own original look.

EXPRESSION SERIES
UPPER PLAYGROUND
Based in San Francisco, California, Upper Playground was founded in 1998. It has become a leader in today's progressive art movement with its innovative apparel line and art gallery, FIFTY24SF.

ANNIVERSARY SERIES
SUPERSTAR 35
Shrouded in mystery, Model 35 was the most sought-after release of the collection. Only 300 pairs were produced, and the only way to obtain one (unless you were very well connected) was through a treasure hunt competition. The shoe is made almost entirely from premium leathers (including the outsole). The white leather box also contained a gold shoehorn, sandalwood lasts and a cleaning kit.

ANNIVERSARY SERIES

| Etched White | Etched Black | Mono | Perforated | Suede | Graphic | Superstar 35 |

For the 2007 release of *The Simpsons Movie*, Vans commissioned 12 urban artists to help create 14 pairs of sneakers. Each artist was invited to give their interpretation of the iconic US cartoon, leading to 14 completely different designs. The artists involved included David Flores, Futura 2000, Gary Panter, Geoff McFetridge, KAWS, Mr. Cartoon, Neckface, Sam Messer, Stash, Taka Hayashi, Todd James and Tony Munoz. Each shoe was limited to 100 pairs.

In return, the creator of *The Simpsons*, Matt Groening, created caricatures of each of the contributing artists. The portraits can be found on shoeboxes created especially for the project.

To celebrate the release of the shoes, Vans and *The Simpsons* put on a launch party and exhibition. On display at the event were original sketches by the artists, skateboard decks emblazoned with Matt Groening's caricatures of the artists and the shoes themselves.

www.thesimpsons.com

VANS
THE SIMPSONS

NECKFACE
Vans Chukka Boot

SAM MESSER
Vans Slip-On

GARY PANTER
Vans Era

FUTURA 2000
Vans Sk8-Mid LX

DAVID FLORES

FUTURA

GARY PANTER

KAWS

MR. CARTOON

NECKFACE

VANS

the SIMPSONS "OFF THE WALL"

VANS

STASH

TAKA HAYASHI

TODD JAMES

GEOFF MCFETRIDGE

SAM MESSER

TONY MUNOZ

TAKA HAYASHI
Vans Sk8-Hi

GEOFF MCFETRIDGE
Vans Chukka Boot

STASH
Vans Mid Skool

TODD JAMES
Vans Sk8-Hi

KAWS
Vans Chukka Boot

MR. CARTOON
Vans Slip-On

DAVID FLORES
Vans Slip-On

DAVID FLORES
Vans Sk8-Hi

TONY MUNOZ
Vans Sk8-Hi

TONY MUNOZ
Vans Slip-On

NIKE AIR U BREATHE

Released in 2006, the Air U Breathe pack from Nike was a quickstrike artist collaboration. The theme of the project was simply Air, and the pack included three different shoes: an Air Max 1 by Ben Drury, an Air Stab by Hitomi Yokoyama and an Air Max 360 by Kevin Lyons. Each designer was also asked to produce a T-shirt and a Windrunner jacket for the project.

UK-based freelance art director and designer Ben Drury (famed for his work with record label Mo' Wax) took his inspiration from the pirate radio scene in London. The shoe features some great details, including the phrase 'Hold Tight' (a reference to the language of pirate radio) embroidered on the tongue and a stitched radio-wave graphic on the heel, while the mudguard of the shoe is made from a 3M Scotchlite reflective material.

Japanese-born Hitomi Yokoyama currently resides in London and designs for the streetwear brands Gimme 5 and GoodEnough UK, as well as collaborating with brands such as Undercover, Mad Hectic, Let it Ride, aNYthing and A Bathing Ape. For the Air U Breathe project, Yokoyama took her inspiration from the lightness and agility of animals such as cats and rabbits – hence the cartoon graphic on the heel.

Kevin Lyons' laser-etched artwork on the Air Max 360 was influenced by three things: Peter Saville's cover art for Joy Division, Fillmore poster art and the flyers of breakbeat DJ Kool Herc. Lyons is a prolific artist and designer who has worked with SSUR, Girl Skateboards, Commonwealth Stacks, HUF, Stussy, adidas, *Tokion Magazine* and BEAMS. He also runs his own experimental studio, Natural Born (www.naturalborn.com).

KEVIN LYONS

HITOMI YOKOYAMA

'The idea behind my design is that Nike Air is so light that it feels as if you are running barefoot. I was thinking of some agile, bouncing animal like a cat or a rabbit, which is where the idea of the paws with shoe laces comes from.'

BEN DRURY

Shown here are two versions of Drury's shoe: a sample version and the final production version. The sample features black-stitched HOLD TIGHT lettering on the tongue instead of silver. 'In the context of pirate radio,' explains Drury, 'HOLD TIGHT is a statement of intent – get ready, prepare yourself. I love the way the atmosphere and excitement of the listener's communion with pirate radio can be distilled into a literal shorthand. The words contain great power and resonance for me as a silent listener.'

Other differences between the sample and production models are that the aerial graphic on the footbed is gloss black on black instead of silver on black, the heel piece is plain black premium leather instead of perforated leather, and the top lace eyelets are 3M Scotchlite instead of black suede.

ADIDAS ADICOLOR

Ahead of its time, the original adicolor concept was launched back in 1983; adidas offered pure white footwear models with specially created quick-drying and weatherproof pens. This innovative approach allowed consumers to produce their very own pair of sneakers.

The concept was relaunched in 2006 by adidas Originals, enhanced by a set of comprehensive, sophisticated customization tools ranging from felt-tip pens to spray paints and more. In addition, adidas expanded the project into a collection of a massive 42 pairs of adicolor shoes. The collection was divided into two major parts, the White Series (featuring six sneakers that referred back to the original customization concept) and the innovative Colour Series (divided into Red, Blue, Yellow, Green, Pink and Black), which featured a number of collaborations with icons from the worlds of fashion, design and art.

Each colour (including the white series) featured six shoes: an adidas adicolor Low, an adicolor High, a Century Low, a Stan Smith and two versions of the Superstar II. The different models were available through various distribution channels, with each sneaker being coded according to the colour series and level of release. For example, R1 was the most limited release of the red series, and B6 was the most widely available release of the Blue series. Adidas also created a range of apparel and accessories for all the collections.

WHITE SERIES

W1
adicolor Low

W2
adicolor High

BLUE SERIES

BL1
Black Tiger Studio for Styles
adicolor Low

BL2
Cey Adams
adicolor High

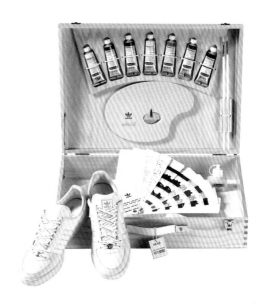

W3
Century Low

W4
Stan Smith

W5
Superstar II

W6
Bill McMullen for
Foot Locker - New York
Superstar II

BL3
Toy2R
Century Low

BL4
Tron
Stan Smith

BL5
Denim
Superstar II

BL6
Bill McMullen for
Foot Locker - Bronx
Superstar II

GREEN SERIES

G1
Jim Lambie for
The Hideout
adicolor Low

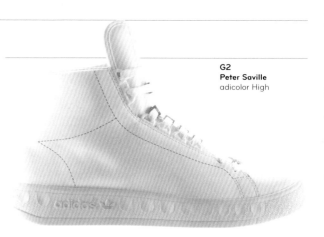

G2
Peter Saville
adicolor High

PINK SERIES

P1
Wood Wood
adicolor Low

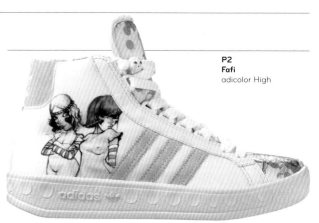

P2
Fafi
adicolor High

BLACK SERIES

BK1
Claude Closky for
Colette
adicolor Low

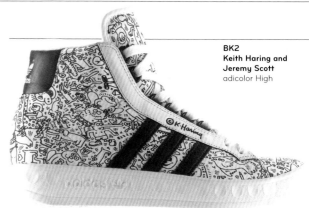

BK2
Keith Haring and
Jeremy Scott
adicolor High

G3
Emilio Pucci
Century Low

G4
Kermit
Stan Smith

G5
Camo
Superstar II

G6
Bill McMullen for Foot Locker - Staten Island
Superstar II

P3
Vice
Century Low

P4
Miss Piggy
Stan Smith

P5
Satin
Superstar II

P6
Bill McMullen for Foot Locker - Brooklyn
Superstar II

BK3
Crooked Tongues
Century Low

BK4
Trimmy
Stan Smith

BK5
Leather
Superstar II

BK6
Bill McMullen for Foot Locker - New York
Superstar II

RED SERIES

R1
J-Money for Dave's
Quality Meat
adicolor Low

R2
Surface To Air
adicolor High

YELLOW SERIES

Y1
HUF
adicolor Low

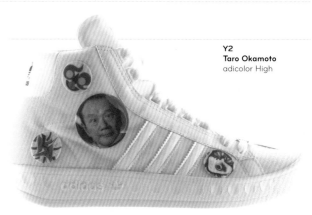

Y2
Taro Okamoto
adicolor High

R3
Dark Horse Comics
Century Low

R4
Betty Boop
Stan Smith

R5
Suede
Superstar II

R6
**Bill McMullen for
Foot Locker -
Manhattan**
Superstar II

Y3
Panini
Century Low

Y4
Mr Happy
Stan Smith

Y5
Monogram
Superstar II

Y6
**Bill McMullen for
Foot Locker - Queens**
Superstar II

As part of the adicolor project, adidas ran a competition in which anybody could submit a customized design of an adicolor White Series collection piece. Adicolor partners Cey Adams, Fafi and Crooked Tongues narrowed the entries down to 20 finalists, who were then put to a public vote. The winner was New York-based Ari Lankin, whose Hokusai design received 20 per cent of the vote. The design was produced in a limited production run of 50, with 25 pairs allocated to Lankin and 25 pairs going on sale to the public.

NIKE LASER PROJECT

Originally starting life in Nike's Innovation Kitchen, the use of a laser was first developed as a way of accurately cutting material. The laser technology itself is nothing new – working in much the same way as a desktop printer, the laser simply plots a course based on computer instructions, burning a pattern that can be incredibly intricate (similar to the technology used in the creation of electronic circuit boards). It was Nike designer Mark Smith who saw past the industrial applications of the technology and realized the potential the process had as a creative tool. In 2003, the Nike Laser Project was born, with Smith asking four artist friends (Tom Luedecke, Stephan 'Maze' Georges, Mike Desmond and Chris Lundy) to help produce six shoes, all of which were to be lasered with specifically created artwork. Smith himself created an Air Force 1 and a Cortez, Luedecke a Cortez, Georges an Air Force 1, Desmond a Dunk Low and Lundy a one-piece Dunk Low.

Depending on the design, the laser works in much the same way as a tattoo gun, with a Line Burn setting for detailed line graphics and a Solid Burn for removing more material and filling in shaded areas.

There is also the ability to combine both of these processes, resulting in a more complicated application of the laser.

Obviously, the graphic artwork had to be based around the architecture of the shoe elements; but incredibly, the drive for the biggest canvas space possible led Smith and Nike to re-engineer a number of shoes, creating uppers made entirely from one piece of (pigskin) leather. This meant that not only did the laser technology change the aesthetic possibilities of the shoe design, but it also improved performance, as less material aids breathability, and means less weight and greater comfort.

The project was launched with an exhibition at the Elizabeth Gallery in New York featuring original artwork and developmental shoe models, as well as the final sneakers themselves.

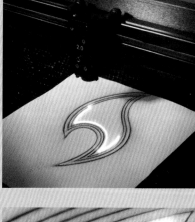

MARK SMITH
Nike Air Force 1
Nike designer and project curator Mark Smith designed this tattoo-inspired Air Force 1. Previously working for Vans and DC Shoes, Smith started his career at Nike in the early 1990s as an apprentice to famed Nike designer Tinker Hatfield.

CHIS LUNDY
Nike Dunk Low (One-Piece)
Surfer and artist (after a serious accident to his
knee, he decided to concentrate on painting),
Lundy applied this flow-inspired artwork to a
one-piece Dunk.

STEPHAN 'MAZE' GEORGES
Nike Air Force 1
New York graffiti artist Maze (who is also part of
Nike's Advanced Concept Team) applied his street-
art style to this Air Force 1.

Mark Smith again worked with laser technology on these Nike Air Jordan IIIs – a special project for basketball superstar Michael Jordan's 40th birthday.

In 2007 Smith also designed these laser etched Nike Fukijama Turtle Air Force 1's for the HBO series *Entourage*. Episode 33 of the show featured lead character Turtle hunting for a pair of sneakers at Los Angeles sneaker store Undefeated. Only a very limited number of pairs were made, and Smith also created a special wooden box with lasered details as part of the project. Shown here is the Fukijama Turtle (black, white and gold) and the Fukijama Undefeated collaboration (blue) that Turtle was hunting for in the show. The writer, director and cast members of the show all received a pair of personally customized Fukijama Turtle shoes - one of these pairs was sold on eBay for $15,100.

www.endtoendproject.com

ADIDAS END TO END

In 2006 adidas, in partnership with Foot Locker, gathered seven of the world's best graffiti artists to create End To End. The project took its name from a graffiti term referring to a train carriage that has been painted from one end to the other. The result is a unique collection of footwear, clothing and accessories available exclusively through Foot Locker.

The concept was to take graffiti artwork from the sketchbook to the streets by giving the artists free rein in a London warehouse for three days. The artists – Smart (Italy), Skore (UK), 123 Klan's Scien (Canada), Can2 and Atom (Germany), Siloette and Rime (US) – were required to start with a blank sketchbook and work through the entire graffiti process, finishing with something that would be incorporated into a sneaker design. Cameras were set up throughout the warehouse to capture the whole design process.

The artists were able to select the shoe models of their choice, and at the end of the three days they then worked with the adidas design team to translate the artwork on to the footwear and apparel pieces. Three pairs of sneakers featuring work by all of the artists were also released. The original artwork, together with a beautifully produced book documenting the project, was showcased on a graffiti-covered bus that toured Europe, stopping at London, Berlin, Milan, Rome, Barcelona and Paris.

The success of the project was revisited in 2007, reuniting the seven artists for a new collection of sneakers (shown next spread) and apparel, featuring clean colours and quality materials.

2006

ATOM/CAN2
Pro Lawn

SMART
Stan Smith

ATOM/CAN2
Centennial

SKORE
Pro Lawn

RIME
Stan Smith

END TO END
Stan Smith

SCIEN
Stan Smith

END TO END
Stan Smith

SILOETTE
Stan Smith

KINGS
Stan Smith

2007

ATOM/CAN2
Rod Laver

ATOM/CAN2
Stan Smith High

RIME
Superskate 2

SCIEN
Decade Lo

SILOETTE
Pro Lawn

SMART
Stan Smith

SKORE
Stan Smith

ALL CITY
Centennial Lo

ALL CITY
Top Ten

KINGS
Forum Mid

www.feiyue-shoes.com

FEIYUE

In 2005, founders of the French collective Seven Dice, Patrice Bastian and Charles Munka, decided to team up with fading Chinese shoe manufacturer Feiyue to relaunch the brand into the modern world. Originally founded in Shanghai in 1920, Feiyue became famous during the 1930s for robustness, flexibility and comfort – making it the shoe of choice for practitioners of the Chinese martial arts.

Feiyue's vintage quality comes from its heritage, a simple Chinese shoe with a century-old origin and history. Seven Dice create different collections each year based on two shoe models, the Feiyue Lo and the Feiyue Hi. They have also collaborated on limited-edition designs with many artists including Shin Tanaka, Bshit and Run 777.

RUN 777
www.777run.com

GRAPHIK DZIGN: THINK GREEN
www.graphik-dzign.com

MOTO 777
www.moto777.com

BLANKDELETER
www.blankdeleter.com

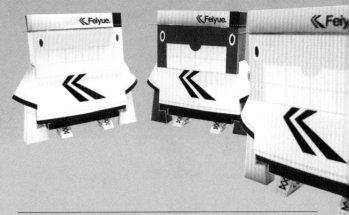

SEVEN DICE: ROCK STAR DREAM
www.feiyue-shoes.com

SHIN TANAKA
www.shin.co.nr

BSHIT
www.bshit.org

LCP UNITED: SIX THOUSAND PROJECT
www.lcp-united.com

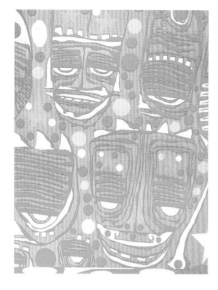
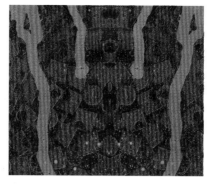

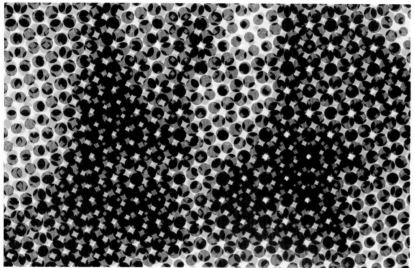

GRAVIS ARTIST FOOTBED SERIES

Many sneaker-based collaborations feature artwork on the insoles, but this is the first and only collection so far that concentrates specifically on this hidden element of sneakers. The foot bed is actually one of the most suitable areas for artwork; it allows the artist/designer the most freedom, as the almost flat canvas doesn't have to concern itself with wearability.

Back in 2001 – the beginning of the current collaboration phenomenon – Gravis asked five urban artists to produce artwork for their Perimeter Support Foot beds (aka insoles). The artists involved – Stash, Futura 2000, SSUR, Kostas Seremetis and Phil Frost – each produced artwork in their own inimitable style. Stash's design featured his now infamous spray-cap pattern, Futura drew on his military past, Seremetis used his Assassin comic-book character, while Frost's artwork featured his stylistic face drawings and SSUR used a photograph of a 1970s glamour model.

Each foot bed came with its own blister pack and card – taking inspiration from collectable toy figure packaging (Star Wars, for instance) – and these limited-edition packs were hand-numbered to add to their collectability.

Sne

Art & Makers

www.ericquebral.com

ERIC QUEBRAL

After completing a fine art degree at university, Eric Quebral decided to incorporate his addiction to sneakers into his art-making. What began as a learning exercise with Photoshop evolved into the layered and cut wood-grain pieces. 'The wood-grain work has been ongoing since late 2002. I call this work Gepetto, as he was the carpenter who carved Pinocchio out of wood.' As well as sneakers, Quebral also creates artwork based on other themes related to pop culture.

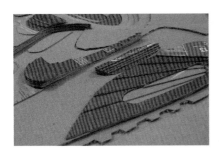

www.davewhite.me.uk

DAVE WHITE

Born in Liverpool, UK, in 1971, Dave White attended art school at the age of 16, and had had his first solo exhibition by the time he was 18. Since then he has exhibited worldwide and has been painting sneakers since 2002. 'I have explored sneakers as a vehicle for my painting as I find them incredible objects to look at. Whether it's the line, the silhouette, colour, shape, form or texture, I believe sneakers are some of the most beautiful things ever designed.' Being on the cover of *Creative Review* in 2003 helped bring his work to world attention and projects with the likes of Nike and New Balance soon followed.

White has been embraced by the phenomenon that is sneaker culture largely thanks to his live painting displays at 'Sneaker Pimps', the world's largest exhibition of sneakers and sneaker-related artwork (see pages 192–195), where he performs in front of audiences of up to 3000 people. White has also recently launched his own clothing brand that includes a large collection of apparel and accessories featuring his sneaker-inspired paintings.

THE COURT'S A BATTLEFIELD

'The Court's A Battlefield', shown both pages, is a series of paintings created especially for the 25th anniversary of the Nike Air Force 1 basketball shoe. The work explores military imagery to celebrate and symbolize the fierce competition that has always existed on the basketball court.

White also made two pairs of custom shoes for the show (one pair shown above left). Both were based on US Navy jet planes that displayed signs of wear and tear from service, much the same as sneakers. 'I used to be obsessed by making models, and making them look worn, rusty and scuffed. I hated the pristine appearance, as it defied the reality'. The shoebox was based on ammunition cases and made to look metallic.

Air Force Carrier, shown left, depicts a US Naval carrier displaying various AF1 colourways on the flight deck, symbolizing the proud collector and their treasured hardware. *Heavy Ammunition*, above, shows a Chinook helicopter struggling to lift an AF1 tank.

Chalked Up Another Pair, shown top, is a piece about sneaker collectors who are always trying to bag that next pair. *Air Force 1*, shown bottom, again depicts the AF1 basketball shoe using military imagery.

White is best known for his trademark sneaker paintings. 'The intent of my work has always been about capturing the character and essence of my subjects. I would say what I do is somewhere between Pop and Expressionism.'

NIKE WET PAINT
In 2005, White worked on the Nike Wet Paint project, a collaboration with Nike to help celebrate the tenth anniversary of the Air Max 95. A pack of neon and grey Air Max sneakers was released, paying homage to the original Air Max 95 colourway. The pack originally included an Air Max 1, Air Max 90 and an Air Stab (which was never released); the AM1 and AM90 were released as a hyperstrike set with a specially designed box, limited-edition prints, stickers and a Tywek jacket. Only 40 sets of each were released.

In 2007 Dave White, pictured below, top left, launched his clothing and accessory brand, a collection focusing on White's sneaker-inspired paintings. The T-shirts are screen-printed more than ten times to capture the depth and surface of the originals – a process that took 18 months to perfect.

www.shin.co.nr

SHIN TANAKA

Graffiti writer and designer Shin Tanaka is Japan's premier paper artist. He started by creating paper templates and models of his favourite sneakers to display on his desk. 'I love sneakers and I wanted to collect them, but I could only display one or two on my desk at a time. However, if I made smaller sneakers I could display many more, so I started making paper sneakers.' Using origami, the ancient Japanese art of paper folding, Tanaka's creations are cut from a carefully constructed template and when made measure approximately 7cm in length.

As well as sneakers, Tanaka also makes paper toy characters, the most famous probably being T-Boy. A selection of these templates (including a Nike Air Force 1 template) is available to download on his website. 'Paper sneakers can be easily customized and many people download the blank template, colour or draw something and make their own designs.'

Above: adidas custom design for the Meister adidas Originals store in Kobe, Japan. Below: Design for the adidas adicolor custom show in Taipei, Taiwan.

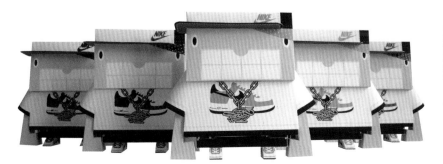

In 2007, Tanaka created a Nike Air Force 1 template for 'Rock, Paper, Scissors', a Nike event held in Cape Town, South Africa. Local designers and artists were then invited to customize the models for the exhibition.

ONITSUKA TIGER

In 2007, Tanaka teamed up with sports fashion brand Onitsuka Tiger to create a unique design that allowed footwear fans to create their own customized origami sneakers. The collaboration – an element of Onitsuka Tiger's Made Of Japan brand campaign – celebrates Japanese creativity and innovation. Tanaka's exclusive origami template of the Onitsuka Tiger Mexico 66 sneaker is available to download at www.onitsukatiger.co.uk. Those who made the sneakers could post an image of their creation on the website; the best design, as judged by Tanaka, received a free pair of Mexico 66 sneakers. The project was commissioned by PR company Mischief, with website design by Carpe Diem.

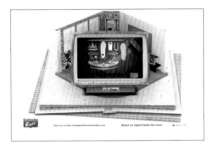
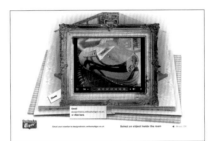
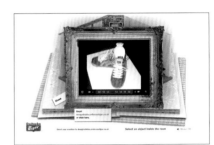

This page: Shown below is an example of the finished design. Continuing the paper art theme, the website that housed the Tanaka project, shown above, was designed to resemble a pop-up book.

Opposite page: The origami template is available to download from the Onitsuka Tiger website.

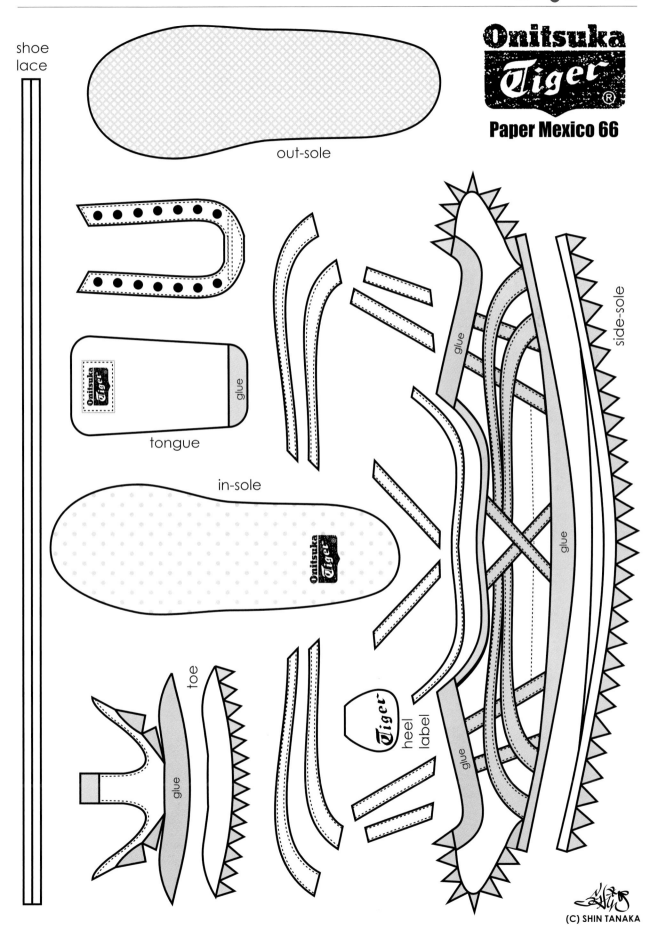

shoe lace

out-sole

Onitsuka Tiger ®

Paper Mexico 66

tongue

in-sole

glue

side-sole

glue

glue

toe

glue

Tiger heel label

glue

(C) SHIN TANAKA

The concept of I Have Pop™ was conceived in 2003 by JUSE, a graffiti artist disillusioned by the medium's conservative nature. His idea was to create a different perspective on particular elements of pop culture through a series of street art projects. These projects could be either a tribute, or a criticism, but the meaning was deliberately left open to the observer. 'The items themselves and the location create the context. Not everyone will be able to understand what is being communicated, but the people who it is intended for will get it.'

By 2004, I Have Pop™ had turned into a reality. For the first project release, JUSE created a series of life-size concrete Nike Dunk sneakers and secretly placed them in front of some of the world's most high-profile sneaker boutiques. Without knowing where these concrete sneakers had come from, some of the stores even took them inside and put them on display. Word of the mysterious project travelled quickly and one year later all was publicly revealed, sparking a huge response.

JUSE is responsible for each project, from plans to production, and personally travels to all destinations for each project's execution and documentation. 'In the course of these projects my frequent-flyer status went from nothing to gold and my bank account the other way around.'

www.ihavepop.com

I HAVE POP™

CONCRETE DUNKS

In 2004, between the months of June and November, Netherlands-based artist JUSE secretly made ten pairs of concrete Nike Dunks and placed them in front of various streetwear stores in North America and Europe. Each pair of Dunks were numbered, and encased within the concrete itself was a card detailing the release date. After the last pair was placed the moulds were destroyed to ensure exclusivity. 'The desired response was to have people wondering what they were and who was behind them. I wanted to create a sense of want, just like Nike does with their limited-edition shoes. I also wanted people to question the limited-edition phenomenon.'

The stores were selected based on their involvement with popular street culture and included UNDFTD (Los Angeles and Santa Monica), Richard Kidd (Vancouver), Nort (New York and Berlin), 90 Square Meters (Amsterdam), Solebox (Berlin), Huf (San Francisco) and Dave's Quality Meat (New York).

STREETWISE

Commissioned in 2006 by Nike for their 'Festival of Air' exhibition in Niketown, London, this piece was created as a tribute to the subcultures that adopted the Nike Air Max 90 and the streets on which it is used. The idea was to make the base of the piece the focal point, rather than the shoes and legs on top of it. The piece also highlights the contrast between the heavy surface materials used on the street and the lightness of the air in the sole of the shoe.

The shoes and legs are made from solid concrete, while the air bubble was created using clear polyurethane resin. The base is made from various pavement and surface materials such as asphalt, bricks, cobblestones and concrete.

THINK OUTSIDE THE BOX
Produced in collaboration with Solebox for the
2006 Berlin and Barcelona exhibition 'Untitled', I
Have Pop™ came up with the idea of creating
sneakers from the boxes they are packaged in.
'Because most of my projects have a critical note, I
dubbed the project Think Outside The Box, hoping
to spur people on to think a little further than the
next cool pair of sneakers.'

www.freedomofcreation.com

FREEDOM OF CREATION

The Electric Tiger Land campaign was created in 2008 by Amsterdam-based advertising agency StrawberryFrog as part of Onitsuka Tiger's Made of Japan brand strategy. The Electric Light Shoe, the focus of the campaign, is a homage to the ambience and energy of Japan. Designed by Dutch agency Freedom of Creation, the one meter long sculpture features a city within a shoe – incorporationg elements from Tokyo's skyline including neon signage, various modes of transport, markets and vending machines. Many of the features are individually lit by one of 300 LED lights and there is also an iPod dock which plays ambient sounds through hidden speakers.

The incredibly detailed shoe was created by FOC designers Janne Kyttanen and Mads Thomsen using rapid-prototyping technology – a type of three dimensional printing which uses successive layers of liquid, powder or sheet material to build a 3-D model. The shoe was then shot by Japanese photographer Satoshi Minakawa.

In addition, StrawberryFrog also produced seven 70cm-long sculptures (two for Germany, one each for France, UK, Korea, Australia and Japan), as well as 15 smaller versions of 40cm in length, to be displayed in stores worldwide.

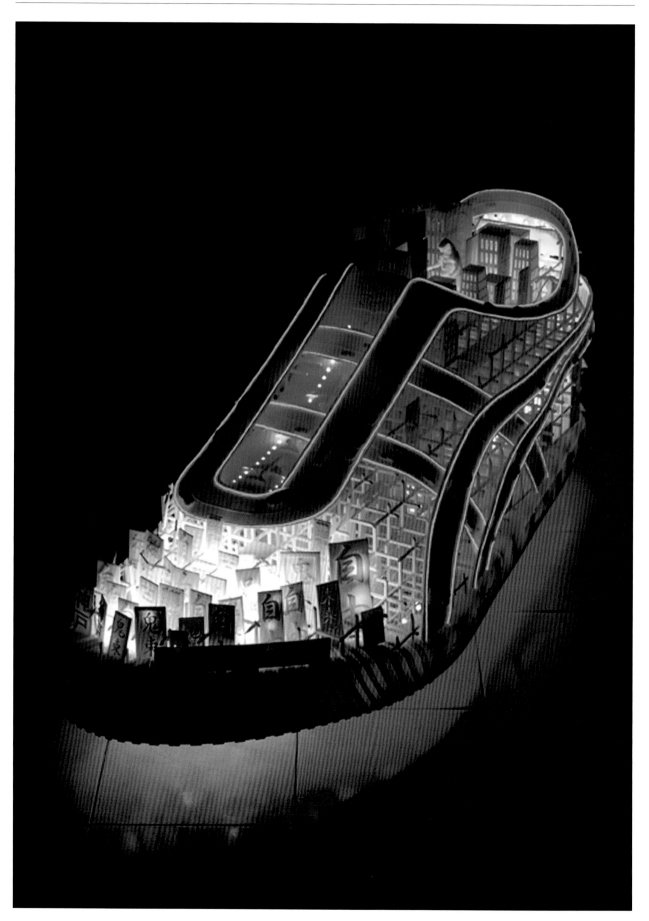

Advertising is usually inspired by product, but ironically in this case a special rendering of the Electric Light Shoe model was created for three limited edition Onitsuka Tiger shoes. The Sunotore 72 models (shown above) incorporate reflective and light-emitting materials in their design. T-shirts using light reflective inks were also produced as part of the project.

www.garybaseman.com

GARY BASEMAN

Los Angeles-based Gary Baseman is an award-winning toy designer, illustrator, artist and Emmy award-winning director. Baseman's work is highly influenced by Japanese culture and he is probably best known for his toys (including Dunces, Fire Water Bunnies and Egg Qees), many of which feature in this creation. Part of Onitsuka Tiger's Made Of Japan campaign, this 150cm-long shoe sculpture is based on the Fabre 74. It is made from Baseman's toys plus Japanese objects such as sushi, origami, lucky cats, noodles and chopsticks, with Koi carp used to make the Onitsuka Tiger stripes.

+41 created this Mini Choco AF1 to celebrate the 25th anniversary of the Nike Air Force 1. Below: Mini Choco Sneakers from +41 in collaboration with Bastien Thibault from the Lausanne-based chocolaterie: Blondel. Production started with three different models: the Nike Dunk, Air Trainer and Blazer.

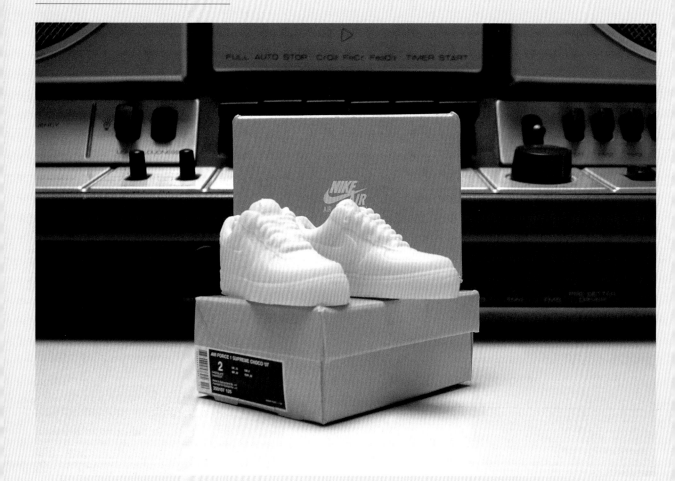

www.plus41.ch

+41

As well as being the international dialling code for Switzerland, +41 is also the fashion and music brand of Swiss graphic design studio //DIY. It was set up in 2001 by Laurence Jaccottet, Ivan Liechti and Philippe Cuendet after the three met while studying at écal (école cantonale d'art de Lausanne) in 1997.

Their first collection was essentially made up of basic T-shirts used as vehicles to convey the group's visual and graphic style. Since then, more collections have been completed and +41 have had the opportunity of creating some exclusive works for numerous brands and designers such as Nike, Apple, Etnies Plus and Colette.

+41 has also expanded its activity into the music business after its creation in 2003 for the release of *Look Ma No Rappers*, a compilation of hip-hop remixes produced by Cuendet, aka MPC.

Before making these life-size chocolate sneakers, +41 got in touch with Bastien Thibault from Blondel chocolaterie. 'He liked the idea and told us it was possible,' explains Cuendet. 'After that we spoke with Nike Switzerland and they got involved and provided us with a pair of sneakers.' Swiss artist and model-maker Denis Biggler then made a plaster mould of the shoes, which was given to Thibault to be thermoformed. The initial result lacked detail, so Biggler suggested making a silicone mould that was far more precise.

THINK FREE

This artwork by Philippe Cuendet for //DIY and +41, was conceived as a kind of ultimate Nike iD, in which existing shoe designs are mutated by combining elements from various sneakers. 'Three artifacts were conceived, as an unlikely triptych, hybrid but not altered; and respectful of a certain consistency that endows bastards with a pedigree.' Interestingly, since this project, Nike themselves have been pushing the boundaries of their designs by creating a range of hybrid concepts such as the One Time Only Air Max 360 sneaker pack from 2006.

This page, right: Starting with a Nike Air Max 180 iD, produced at the Nike Spirit Room in Berlin, Cuendet simply added a Nike Free sole while keeping the 180° cushioning on the heel. Below: A Nike Air Jordan V upgraded with elements of the Jordan IV and mounted on a Nike Free sole.

Opposite page: Nike Air Trainer with a Free sole and mesh panel from the Air Jordan IV.

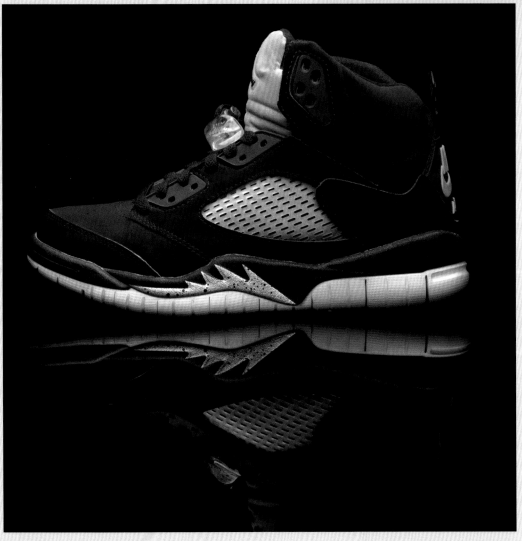

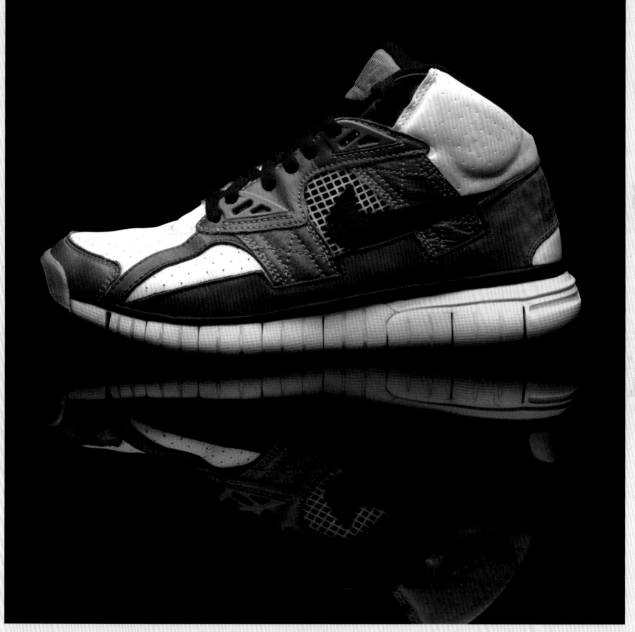

+41 NIKE iD AIR MAX

Produced in 2006, the +41 Nike iD Air Max was a numbered series of 41 pairs and came in a drinks-straw style package, which contained a pair of +41 Nike iD Air Max 1's, a +41 Air Max 1 artwork T-shirt and a pack of sticker eyes.

By personalizing the sneakers with eyes, +41 had the intention of switching traditional roles: instead of people looking at the sneakers, it's the sneakers that look at you. Also, the shoe represents Nike's vision in terms of what they've accomplished: 'A revolutionary system that brought something new and crazy to sports technology,' explains +41, 'and definitely changed the game of the sneaker scene. The artwork +41 created represents these aspects with a glass of sparkling soda full of air bubbles, shoes and history ... and when the air bubbles go through the straw, they turn into eyes.'

Sold out before they were even released, the shoes were only available at the Thomas I Punkt store in Hamburg, with all benefits going to a children's charity. There was a last chance to purchase a pair through the +41 Nike iD Air Max 1 Christie's auction in Zürich (the first time ever Christie's had auctioned a pair of sneakers), with proceeds going to Schtifti, a Swiss charity promoting health for young people through freestyle sports. Five pairs were auctioned, with the highest price reaching 1000 euros.

STRESS NIKE iD AIR FORCE 1

Designed by +41 in collaboration with Swiss rapper Stress, only 15 pairs of these sneakers were made. The shoe was designed in 2007 for 'A Journey Of Force', the Zürich event for the 25th anniversary of the Nike Air Force 1.

ETNIES PLUS

+41 also collaborated with Etnies Plus for this release in 2007. The project included two versions of the Welldon High model (one men's and one women's). The white (women's) shoe features an overall print of various +41 bitmapped icons. Only 289 pairs of the men's and 167 pairs of the women's shoes were available worldwide.

www.nashmoney.com

NASH MONEY

London-based sneaker customizer Nash Money experiments with construction and deconstruction rather than simply applying painted patterns or colourways. He is best known for his Nike customizations, where he applies a moccasin-style stitch to the toe and adds other features like embroidery and coloured stitching. 'It's all done with one leather needle and the iron tips of my fingers – well they fell like iron now anyway,' says Nash.

Always thinking about new projects, not just towards sneaker customizaton but design in general, one of Nash's latest customs has seen him create a bike seat using an Atmos Nike Free Trail 5.0 shoe. According to Nash 'I always have constant pressure to improve my skills and push the boundaries with every custom I make. I'd like to think this is evident since I started in 2004.'

The Afro Centricity Pack was commissioned by Nike for their Festival Of Air celebrations in 2006. The brief was to choose two pairs of sneakers from the Air Max range and customize them in the theme of the era they were originally released. Nash chose the Air Max 1, as he wanted to create an Afro-centric themed custom. As he explains, 'The late 1980s and early 1990s saw a huge focus on Afro-centric culture. This was demonstrated in music, film, television and fashion.' The first pair (below) was based on the *Fresh Prince of Bel Air* television programme and the second pair (above) were inspired by Native Tongues – a collective formed of the biggest hip-hop groups and artists of the time, such as De La Soul, A Tribe Called Quest and the Jungle Brothers.

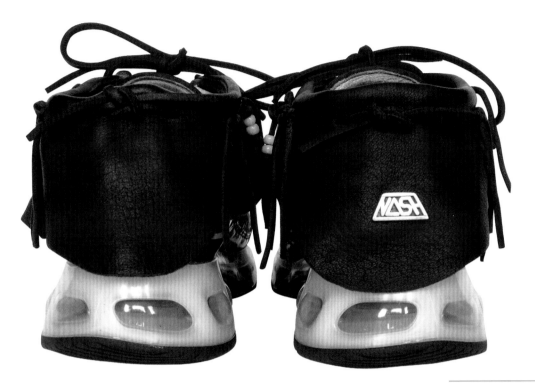

This handstitched model combines a Visvim FBT with an Nike Air Max 360. 'The Visvim FBT has to be one of the most dapper shoes ever,' says Nash, 'with its clean lines and that distinct skirt detailing. Then you have the Air Max 360, with its incredible air unit ingenuity and engineering. It made perfect sense to combine these two in a hybrid.'

www.insaland.com

INSA

After being a well-known name on the London graffiti scene for more than ten years, INSA has now established himself as an artist in his own right. He is probably most recognized for his Graffiti Fetish work, which explores the idea of graffiti/art as an obsession and uses the traditional fetishistic image of the high heel as a recurring motif.

INSA first used this motif on a graffiti piece in which he spelled his name in heels. 'To me the high heel began to represent the ideas I was having about graffiti being an obsession, and it became a symbol of the graffiti fetish I was controlled by.'

Drawing parallels from the fetishistic nature of high heels, INSA's work also focuses on sneakers and sets out to explore the fetish many people, including INSA himself, have for these objects of desire. 'Heels are more of a sexual fetish, but sneakers are a consumer fetish – the only real satisfaction is to buy them and continue this by owning more and more. This fascinates me as in our society so many of our wants and needs are being replaced by consumerism.'

FESTIVAL OF AIR
Custom-made Nike Air Max 90 corset and matching Air Max 90 sneakers for the 'Festival of Air' exhibition at Niketown London, 2006. Photography by Emma Slater.

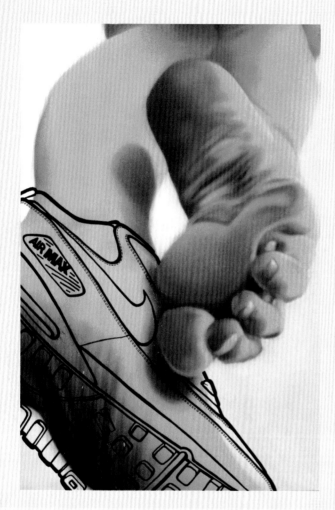
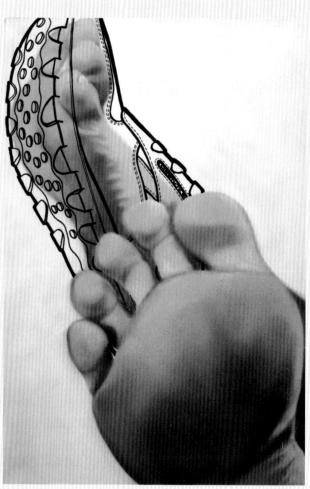

SNEAKER FETISH
Spray paint and marker on canvas, 90 x 120cm. In
this collection of work, INSA displays his technical
skills by using the relatively clumsy media of
marker and spray paints to question his
relationship with objects of consumer fetishism.
'Fetishism to me represents a desire inside us that
is beyond our own control. I like exploring the key
elements that signify these fetishes and applying
them to other areas of desire in our lives, whether
they be natural, like our need for creativity, or
forced on to us, like consumerism.'

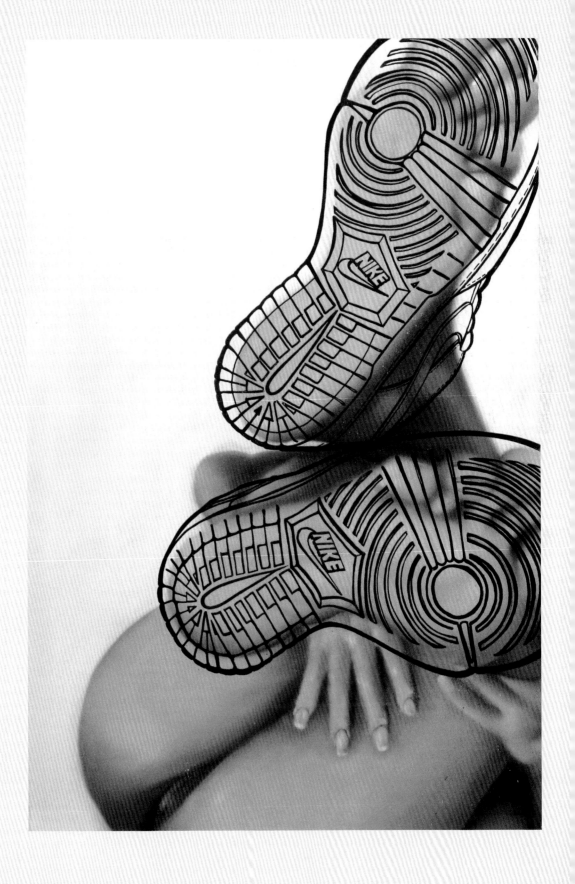

PREMIUM DUNKS
Black on black hand-flocked artwork, with 22-carat gold leaf swooshes, solid gold BEST and INSA lace locks displayed in a bulletproof case. Made to mark INSA's first New York exhibition in 2006.

Postcard from INSA's 'Graffiti Fetish Set One' postcard pack, released at his first solo exhibition in 2005.

DUNK ETHEL
Created in 2005, these one-off custom-painted Dunks (above) were named after INSA's graffiti partner and girlfriend.

PINK GREY DUNK
Shown right is one of three pairs of custom-painted Dunks created in 2005 as a follow-up to the Dunk Ethel. All photography by Emma Slater.

SIBALOM

This is the first in a series of dioramas for Pointer Footwear. It's a depiction of a beautiful, almost untouched rainforest, which has begun to be cut down. Little do the loggers know that they have disturbed an ancient and sacred place containing a giant flower-beast.

JAHRA

This is the second of the Pointer Footwear dioramas. 'There is an oil refinery owned and operated by Black Sun Industries. A helicopter from the refinery has crashed into the pipeline, causing an oil spill which has manifested itself as a huge oil monster about to attack the refinery.'

www.jethrohaynes.com

JETHRO HAYNES

Jethro Haynes is a London-based illustrator, designer and model-maker whose work uses a diverse selection of artistic approaches – textile prints, photographs, hand-drawn posters and paintings, to name but a few.

Inspired by the world, his imagination and his love of model-making, Haynes has built up a fertile working relationship with London-based Pointer Footwear, creating art pieces and advertising for the company. He starts with the shoes themselves: 'They are the blank canvas, and different shoes lend themselves to different styles of landscape; for example, a mountainous environment is more appropriate for a high-top sneaker.'

Working in conjunction with design studio Hudson-Powell, Haynes creates the dioramas to roughly 1/500th scale, as the starting point is always a UK size 8 shoe. They are extremely time-consuming to make, as a large number of the parts have to be handcrafted or sourced from a local model shop. 'We always manage to make everything really difficult for ourselves,' says Haynes, 'by having ideas that once spoken of can't be overlooked.'

DOOMSDAY ASTEROID 2004 MN4
This diorama is set in space. Humans are trying to destroy the asteroid before it reaches Earth, but inside the rock lies a beast with other ideas.

WALTER
This sculpture of a liquid-based life form spurting out of a pipe and turning into humanoid form was used as an advertisement for Pointer Footwear. This life-size sculpture is made almost entirely from expanding foam.

This collage was created for an article on Pointer Footwear in Lodown Magazine. The shoe represents an experimental submarine that has malfunctioned, contaminating the surrounding sea-life and causing it to mutate.

THE POINTER ART COLLECTIVE
Pointer's Art Collective is a series of publications created in association with Pointer Footwear. The idea behind the collective is to document and display artwork that has influenced and inspired those behind the Pointer brand. Shown above is the boxed set of the first four publications, The Side Effects of Urethane, The Blank Tape Spillage Fete, Saving Up To Become An Octopus (which is dedicated to the work of Haynes) and Awaken! Slumber Maps And Giffle.

www.rockwellclothing.com

PARRA

Parra (aka Pieter Janssen) is an Amsterdam-based artist whose work blurs the boundaries between illustration, graphic design and calligraphy. His artwork features a mix of bold flat colour, hand-rendered typography, strange bird-like creatures and voluptuous female forms. Mostly self-taught, Parra has produced commercial work for companies such Nike, Etnies, Heineken and Ben & Jerry's, as well as more underground work for the likes of record label Rush Hour, sneaker store Patta and skateboard company Zoo York. Parra is also the creative force behind Rockwell clothing, a line of apparel featuring his trademark imagery.

Parra created this series of Nike Air Max illustrations for a piece entitled 'Art And Science' in the October 2006 issue of Dazed And Confused magazine. The back cover of the magazine (shown above) featured Parra's rendering of an Air Max 360, complete with transparent air bubbles. Art direction was by Peter Stitson.

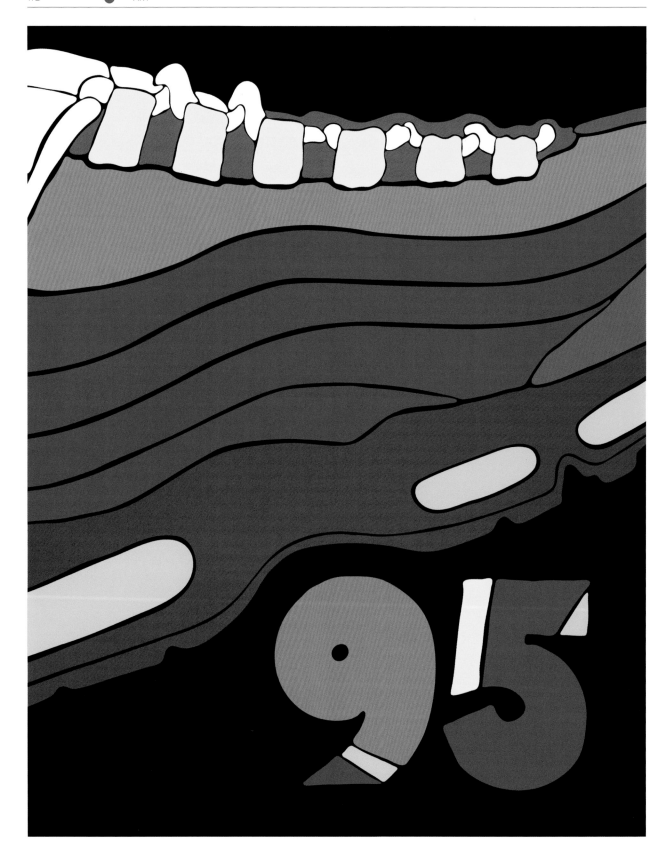

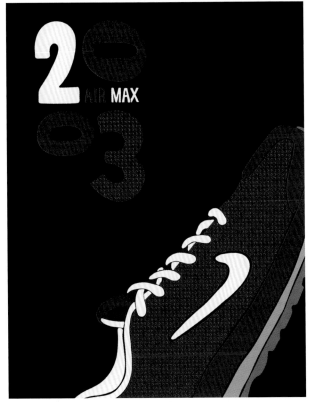

ETNIES PLUS

In 2007, Parra collaborated with Etnies Plus on these two premium sneakers. The men's shoe features flat pink, blue and purple panels with a patent leather tongue. The women's shoe is plain white, with a mix of micro-perforated and mock crocodile skin leathers. Two co-branded T-shirts were also produced as part of the collaboration.

NIKE

Parra is undoubtedly most famous in the sneaker world for his Air Max 1 Amsterdam collaboration with Nike in 2005. Created for Nike's Capital Series (also see page 16), the first colourway was based on Holland's Albert Heijn supermarket corporate colours (initially Parra also wanted to create carrier bags for the release). The shoe was never produced as the supermarket chain changed its colour scheme to blue and white (from orange, blue and white). Parra then changed the design to the now infamous Red Light District colourway, featuring the famous Airmax Girl illustration on the insole. Only 220 pairs of the (quickstrike) shoe were released worldwide; 24 pairs of a hyperstrike version, featuring Parra's embroidered signature, were also created.

www.julesdavid.com

JULES DAVID

Amsterdam-based Jules David Design was founded in 2005 by Julien Rademaker. Inspired by his favourite sneakers, Rademaker created these prints to highlight their shapes, textures and colours. 'I think some of these shoes are a work of art,' says Rademaker, 'a unique piece of design perfectly shaped and beautifully composed. I wanted to play with that idea and change the composition into a new abstract form by using the parts of the shoe I liked the most.'

Nothing is added to the original shoes; elements of the existing designs are simply emphasized to turn them into beautiful abstract patterns.

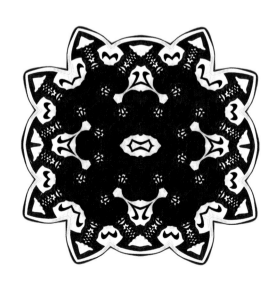

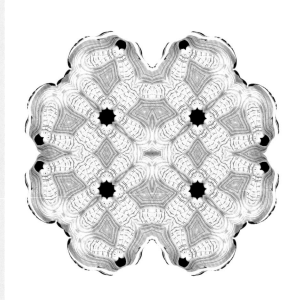

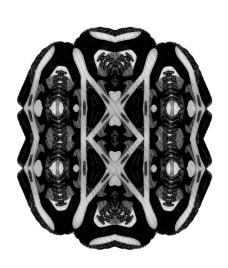

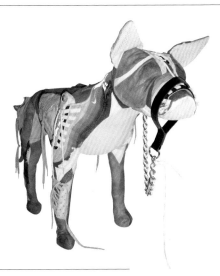

www.vintiandrews.com

VINTI ANDREWS

Vinti Andrews is a London-based fashion designer, whose work cross-references various cultures, including the UK's rich historic past. In 2006, Andrews was invited to participate in the Festival of Air, an event held at London's Niketown celebrating three decades of Nike Air Max. The brief was to represent the history of the Air Max sneaker within British youth street culture. 'We chose the Air Max 95 model as it meant a lot to me – it was a groundbreaking design that totally stood out. I used to hang around Portobello market and was one of the first wearing the green neon colourway – you just couldn't get hold of them.'

The idea of choosing to make the pit bull dogs came from the British phenomenon of 'one man and his dog'. 'We added a twist to this idea by choosing the pit bull species to give our project bite and to represent the aggressiveness and strength of Nike. Also, the only dogs where I live seem to be hybrid pit bull breeds – it wouldn't sit right if we made Nike poodles!' Vinti Andrews selected the sneakers according to colour, design and, most importantly, the cultural significance of the models and how they reflect changing times.

REINO

Reino grew up around his father's jewellery shop – Soho's infamous The Great Frog. After completing an engineering degree, Reino returned to continue the family tradition: 'The shop has been around since 1972, so there is a lot of history of jewellery design and production in my family. I used to hang out there as a kid, learning all the metals and stones, so I guess it was natural that I would follow in my father's footsteps and make jewellery.'

Reino's obsession with sneakers began when he was just ten or eleven – around the time the first Nike Air Max was released. Combining this interest with his passion for jewellery was an obvious step: 'I wanted to interpret sneakers in my own way and to pay homage to the designs and sneakers I loved.' The pieces are handmade to order, and can be solid silver, 24-carat gold-plated or produced in any metal, with any stone of your choice.

Reino has also produced sneaker jewellery for the likes of Crooked Tongues (pages 34–39) and sneaker customizer Nash Money (pages 158–159).

www.arkitip.com

ARKITIP

Founded in Los Angeles in 1999 by Scott Andrew Snyder, *Arkitip* is a unique magazine that publishes specially created artwork by contemporary artists. Every issue is hand-numbered and sold in limited quantities, with some issues coming packaged with art-inspired accessories, like Kevin Lyons-designed coasters or a Phil Frost inflatable graphic ball.

Limited to an edition of 1000, issue 0019 was poly-bagged with a set of mini paper do-it-yourself Nike Safari sneakers, including a set of Arkitip/Nike laces.

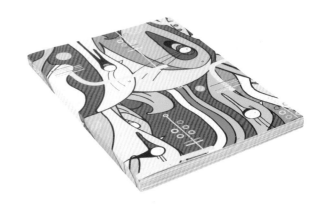

www.rojo-magazine.com

ROJO®AIR

ROJO is a quarterly magazine of images without words. Based in Barcelona and São Paulo, the magazine has a huge network of artists who are often called upon to contribute to various themed projects, including one-off concept magazines like *ROJO®air*. Packed with photographs, illustrations and graphic design pieces, *ROJO®air* is an exclusive limited printed edition, featuring new artwork by 30 artists using Nike Air Max sneakers as inspiration.

Sixeart for *ROJO®air*

Nano4818 for *ROJO®air*

Neasden Control Centre for *ROJO®air*

Dalek for *ROJO®air*

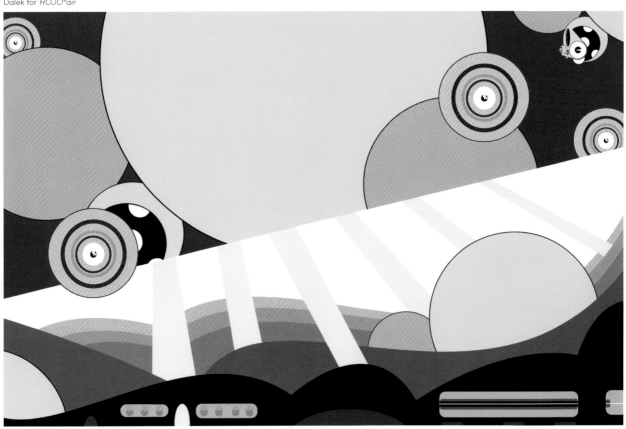

Sosaku Miyazaki for *ROJO®air*

310k for *ROJO®air*

Albert Bertolin for *ROJO®air*

Jemma Hostetler for *ROJO®air*

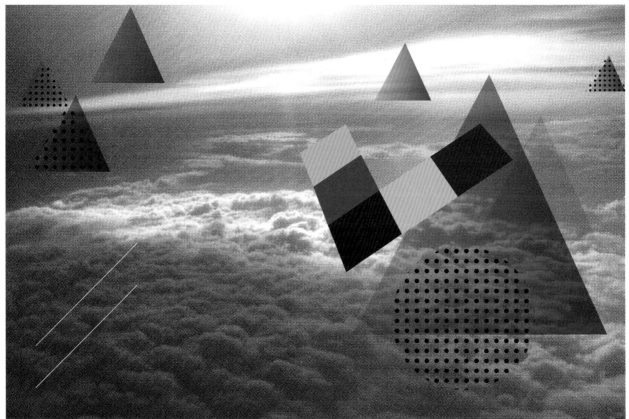

Meomi for *ROJO®air*

Filipe Mesquita for *ROJO®air*

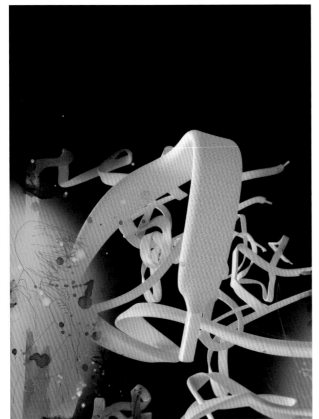

Javier Tles for *ROJO®air*

www.sosu.co.jp

MIHARA YASUHIRO

The collaboration between Puma and Japanese fashion designer Mihara Yasuhiro began in 2000 with the launch of their revolutionary sneaker collection. Since then the partnership has regularly brought together innovative design and a wealth of influences from Japanese culture, resulting in a fresh and vibrant contemporary sneaker collection.

In 2006, to celebrate this collaboration, Puma and Mihara released the limited-edition *Collector's Book* showcasing artwork inspired by the Puma Mihara collection. The artwork was created by four well-known Japanese artists: painter Akira Yamaguchi, contemporary floral sculptor Makoto Azuma, poet Sandaime Uotake and innovative cartoonist Takao Saito.

A beautiful testimonial to the work of Mihara Yasuhiro and Puma, the book also acts as a visual archive documenting the Puma Mihara sneaker styles from the first MY-1 shoe to the most recent addition of the MY-27 for Spring/Summer 2007.

ART WORK *by Makoto Azuma*

ART WORK *by Akira YAMAGUCHI* 山口晃 夕景図

そこには もう
赤とんぼのすきな
おれはいない。

いるのは おやじの
血をひく狼の……
飢えに目をぎらつかせた
狼のすだだけ
なのだ……

Every drop of human emotion has in me...

Instead, what's left is a wolf carrying on his father's blood.
Two wolves, eyes shining with hunger .

In conjunction with the book launch, Puma Mihara
introduced the MY-1 Peace and the MY-9 Love,
limited edition reissues of two of the most innovative
designs from the Puma Mihara sneaker archive.

www.sneakerpimps.net

SNEAKER PIMPS

'Sneaker Pimps' is a touring sneaker show that features rare, limited-edition, vintage, celebrity-signed and artist-collaboration sneakers, plus a collection of sneaker-inspired artwork, fashion and photography. Among other things, the show features a display of more than 1500 sneakers, live hip-hop by world-famous and up-and-coming DJs/MCs, art installations, free running, skateboarding, beat-boxing, ice sculpting and sneaker customization competitions.

One of the biggest attractions of 'Sneaker Pimps' is the live painting and sneaker customizing that takes place at each show; artists of various media paint sneakers and/or canvases in front of thousands of onlookers. The show has featured original works from some of the scene's best artists: Stash, Doze, Shepard Fairey, Mr. Cartoon, Dave White, Cope2, Methamphibian and SBTG among many others.

'Sneaker Pimps' has visited more than 62 cities in countries including Australia, New Zealand, USA, Japan, Singapore, Taiwan, Korea, China, Thailand, Canada, Belgium and The Philippines, making it easily the world's largest sneaker and street-art exhibition.

JB CLASSICS SP-1

'Sneaker Pimps' and JB Classics linked up in 2006 to design and develop the JB SP-1. Limited to just 120 pairs worldwide and using the JB-Peddler Model as the base, the trademark chain-link graphic of 'Sneaker Pimps' was incorporated as the main feature of the design. The sole was created by melting together random blocks of coloured rubber, so each pair produced has a unique colour ratio.

JB CLASSICS SP-2

In 2007, 'Sneaker Pimps' and JB Classics reunited for the JB SP-2, this time using the JB-Getlo Mid model. The colour make-up follows the black and white standards used on the first version, with the addition of a multiple-colour speckled texture.

Individually hand-numbered and packaged with a certificate of ownership, both collaborations were released globally through JB Classics retailers as well as being available at 'Sneaker Pimps' events.

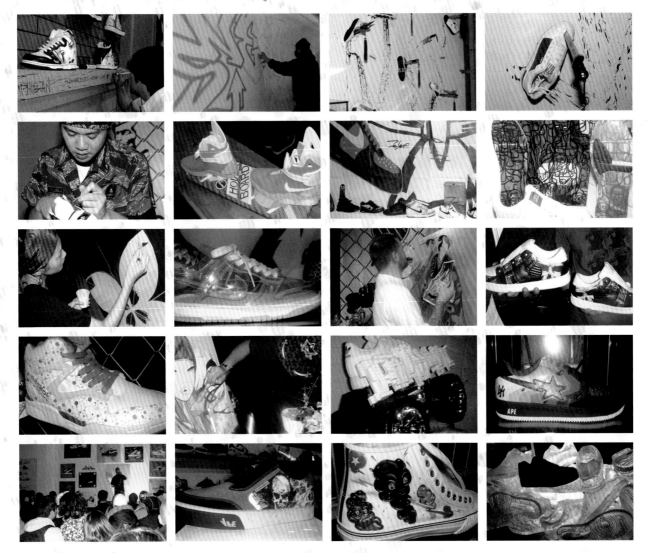

www.johnbaldwin.net

JOHN BALDWIN

In 2000, Lancashire-born artist John Baldwin created these paint-encrusted sneakers for an exhibition in London in collaboration with adidas. Baldwin's art was applied directly to the shoes, which were then turned into photographic prints displaying the high colours and textural surfaces of the paint.

To capture the images, Baldwin used photographic microscopes at London's Tate Gallery's Department of Conservation, which allowed him to develop images that withstood great magnification, giving the prints a particularly intense quality.

For the exhibition, the images were then displayed alongside the original painted shoes.

DIVA Eisaku Kito

www.whitedunk.com

WHITE DUNK

How does an object and what it represents inspire you? What form would that inspiration take using your imagination and creative skills as an artist? What paths would different creative minds take from the same starting point? These are the questions that Nike CEO Mark Parker asked a diverse group of Japanese artists, including animators, illustrators, toy-makers, graphic designers, model-makers and comic writers. Each was given the brief to respond to an unlikely source of inspiration; a white Nike Dunk basketball shoe.

The exhibition 'White Dunk: Evolution Of An Icon' takes its name directly from the point of reference. In American basketball towards the end of the 1970s, an exciting new technique had emerged on the court popularly known as the slam-dunk. Nike began designing sports shoes that they hoped would become synonymous with this phenomenon and, inspired by their already successful Air Jordan and Air Force, Nike debuted the Dunk in 1985.

The 'White Dunk' exhibition opened in Tokyo in early 2004 (with the exterior of the venue designed to look like a Nike Dunk SB silver shoebox), before moving to Paris and finally to Los Angeles in 2005. Photography by Harry Peccinotti.

ORIGINAL PIECE Jun Goshima

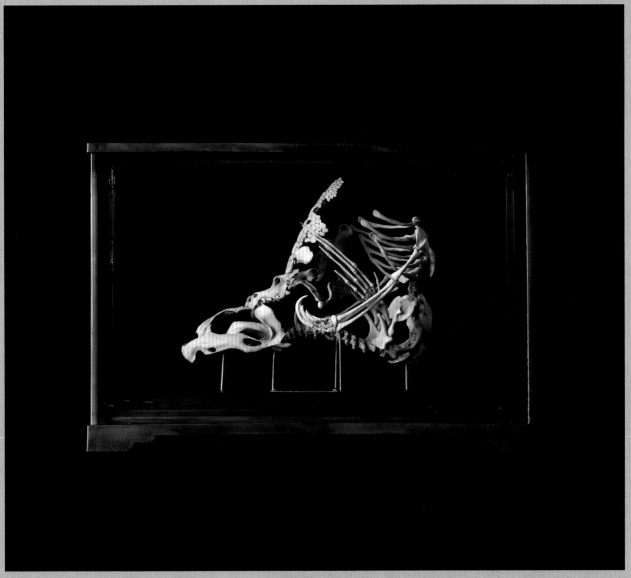

NIKEMAN Keiichi Sato

DOUBLE DUNK Masakazu Katsura

MY DOUBLE DUNK Junichi Taniguchi

UNTITLED Hitoshi Yoneda

FIREBALL Kow Yokoyama

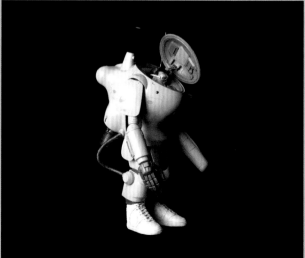

RAKUGAKI DUNK Katsuya Terada

WHITE DUNK EX Naoki Sato

UNTITLED Shinichi Yamashita

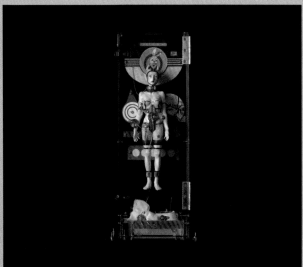

VEHICLE FOR BUDDHA Hideaki Hirata

VAMPIRE UV Yasushi Nirasawa

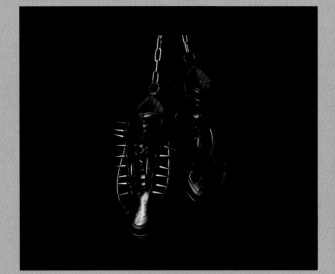

DEFENSE!! Yoshikazu Yasuhiko

MY WHITE DUNK Atsushi Kamijyo

UNTITLED Eiji Nakayama

UNTITLED Yuji Oniki

UNTITLED Yukio Fujioka

DUNK MOVE Haruo Suekichi

NIKE GODDESS Hajime Sorayama

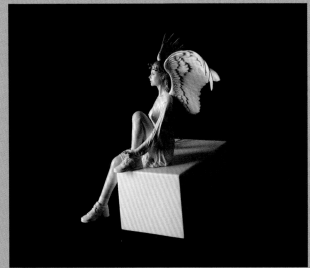

LET'S DUNK Yasuhito Udagawa

NIKE ROBOT Shuji Yonezawa

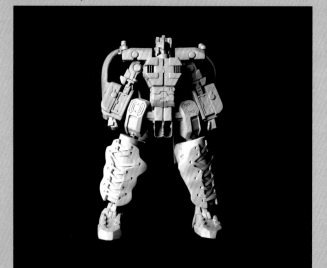

FARMER Takayuki Takeya

PATH TO THE SKY Kenji Ando

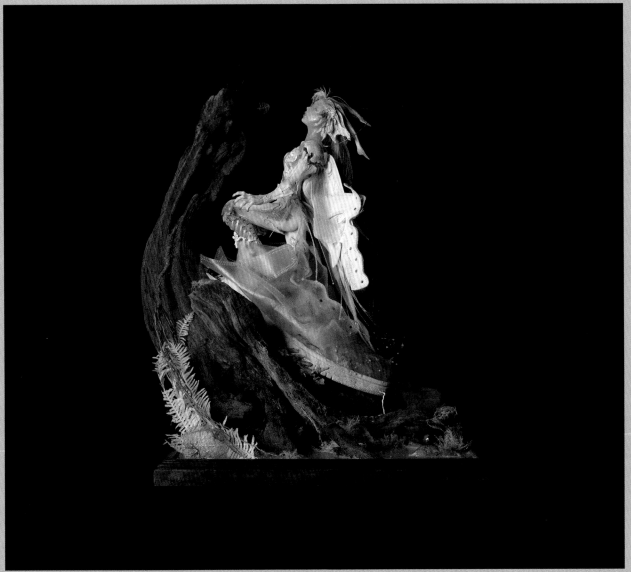

UNTITLED Yukihiro Suzuki

90x90

In 2006, Ido de Voos (of Amsterdam-based store 90 Square Meters) teamed up with photographer Yamandu Roos and stylist Clyde Semmoh to create a concept and exhibition highlighting the diversity of people who wear the Nike Air Max 90 on the streets of Holland. 'The shoe lives among many different cultures and subcultures. It knows no colour, no race and no religion.'

For the first stage of the project, Roos captured various Air Max 90 aficionados with a series of photographs. The pictures were used as a starting point for a group of eight artists each to create their own interpretation of the shoe.

The artists involved included Dutch graffiti legend Delta, JUSE from I Have Pop™, Riëlle Beekmans and Leon Perlot, Russell Maurice of Gasius, News, Pane, Woes van Haaften and Patty Bleumink.

For the exhibition, held at 90 Square Meters, the photographs and artwork were displayed together and a one-off Nike Air Max 90 iD shoe was created for each exhibit. Both the artwork and the shoes were available to purchase on the night.

Nike became involved during the creation of the exhibition, and the artwork from '90x90' eventually became part of 'Run on Air: Seven Cities (Seven Shoes), Seven Stories' – a celebration of three decades of Nike research and development into air-cushioning technology. 'Run On Air' was a creative project combining artists, illustrators, sculptors and filmmakers from Paris, Amsterdam, Berlin, Barcelona, London, Milan and Istanbul.

Photographer Yamandu Roos produced these photographs to document the diversity of people wearing the Nike Air Max 90 shoe. The images were the starting point of the project and served as the inspiration for the artists involved.

Dutch graffiti legend Delta used the name of the
shoe and his 3-D style to create this intricate
typographic sculpture.

Riëlle Beekmans and Leon Perlot interpretated the Air Max 90 in Delfts Blue porcelain.

JUSE, of I Have Pop™, took his inspiration from street football (Panna); the result is an amazing concrete table-football game.

For this piece, entitled *Cavern Biosphere*, Russell Maurice took the ultimate symbol of Air Max and created a mini-city existing among the caverns of the Air Max 90 cushion bubble. 'I like the idea of the nano-city, a tiny microcosmic biosphere existing in this minute encapsulated area of oxygen and space.'

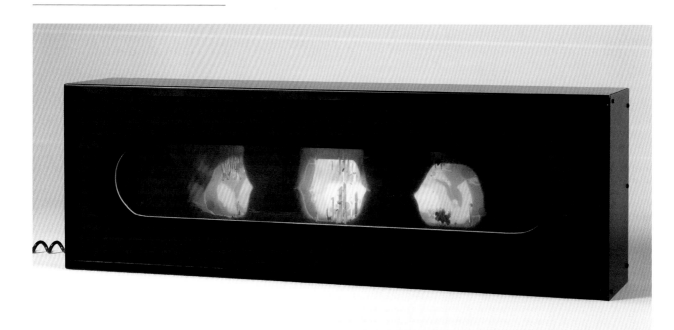

For this piece, entitled *Air Mix*, Woes van Haaften
took his inspiration from mobility, sport and the
urban lifestyle to reinterpret a classic Dutch symbol
– the bike.

Uribe's art-making is a labour-intensive and repetitive process; 'Human Nature' used 25,000 shoelaces, 1500 shoes and 22,000 metal screws.

www.federicouribe.com

FEDERICO URIBE

In 2007, the Chelsea Art Museum in New York was home to Federico Uribe's 'Human Nature' exhibition. The rainforest installation consisted of animal, insect, plant and landscape sculptures produced solely from Puma shoes. 'When I started working with shoes I could not avoid thinking where they came from and all the materials from nature that we use to comfort our life. So as a tribute to what nature gives us all, I got the idea of reconstructing nature from its own raw materials.'

This creative collaboration between Uribe and Puma formed as a result of Uribe's interest in working with everyday objects. From his early work in painting, Columbian-born Uribe evolved into a sculptor using found objects like babies' bottle teats, coins and screws, along with industrial cleaning products and things gathered in street markets.

DEREK ALBECK www.derekalbeck.com

COLE GERST www.option-g.com

JOPHEN STEIN www.jophenstein.com

www.vansskygallery.com

VANS SKY GALLERY

In 2007, Vans undertook the Sky Gallery art programme in Los Angeles, bringing together six of the area's top emerging and recognized art talents by featuring their original work on a prominent billboard in the city. The six artists' work appeared for two months at a time, culminating in a group show at a local gallery at the end of the year. Each artist also created a custom pair of Vans shoes as part of the event.

Additionally, in a bid to give something back to the city that had been such an inspiration to both the company and the artists, Vans made a US$1000 donation to the local charity of each artist's choice.

MARCO ZAMORA www.rtystapparel.com

SAGE VAUGHN www.sagevaughn.com

KELSEY BROOKES www.kelseybrookes.com

www.tomy.com

NIKE TRANSFORMERS

For the release of the *Transformers* movie in 2007, Takara Tomy got together with Nike Japan to produce these shape-changing sneakers. Based on the Nike Free 7.0, the models were available in the guises of Convoy, the Japanese name for Optimus Prime, commander of the Autobots, and Megatron, the leader of the evil Decepticons. A version of Convoy with a marine colourway was also released.

At approximately 13cm in length, the models feature amazing detail and even have real laces connected to the top of the shoe. As a finishing touch, each character is also sporting a miniature pair of Nike Free 7.0 sneakers.

Nike also released this Transformers Pack (shown below) of actual sneakers in 2007. The pack featured an Air Trainer III, an Air Max 90 Boot and an Air Trainer Huarache.

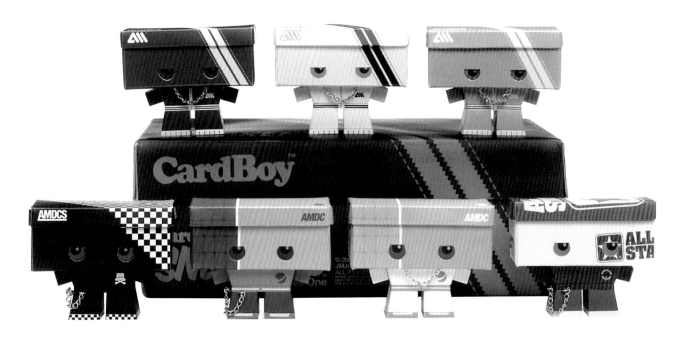

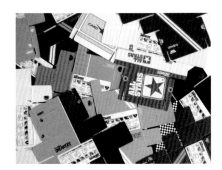

www.cardboy.tv

MARK JAMES

CardBoy was created and designed by graphic artist Mark James as an answer to the dilemma of what to do with the box. When opened, the packaging of this mini-figure transforms into the head of the character. 'I've always designed characters, and collected a few, but the idea of actually making my own figure was something I'd always wanted to do. The cost of getting something made wasn't an option at the time, so I started developing cardboard figures.'

CardBoy Sneakers is the second in the CardBoy series and pays homage to classic sneaker boxes. It features eight characters (each one comes with its own accessories) and is blind-box packaged with one limited chase figure. A limited-edition eight pack was also released containing all eight characters, with the packaging turning into a 200 per cent Sneakers figure.

NIKE SB THREE
BE@RBRICK PROJECT

In 2006, Nike SB teamed up with Japanese toy manufacturer Medicom to produce these Be@rbrick figures as part of the Nike SB Three Be@rbrick Pack – a trio of sneakers including a (baby bear) Dunk Low, a (mummy bear) Dunk Mid, and a (daddy bear) Dunk High. All three of these unique shoes were manufactured using teddy bear fur material.

The Be@rbrick figures, which featured a rendering of a Dunk toecap on their body, were produced in the same colourway as their respective sneakers: the smallest Be@rbrick (50 per cent) is the same colourway as the Dunk Low; the medium size (100 per cent) matches the Dunk Mid; and the largest Be@rbrick (400 per cent) is the same as the Dunk High.

MICHAEL LAU

Artist and toy designer Michael Lau is widely credited as the pioneer of the urban toy movement. His figures form ever-growing urban tribes, such as the Gardeners and Crazy Children, and are famed for their reflections of global street culture.

In 2004, Lau designed 100 sneaker-based figures for an exhibition in his own Hong Kong gallery. Based on the Nike Air Force 1, the Mr. Shoe (Sample) character is a hard-edged and roughly sculpted creation that was created to reflect Lau's design philosophy; that although there is one mould, each shoe takes on its own personality and chooses its own audience. Lau hand-painted each figure, taking inspiration from his favourite design and pop culture references, including fashion brand Hermès, Stanley Kubrick's cinematic masterpiece *A Clockwork Orange*, and the work of contemporary artist Damien Hirst.

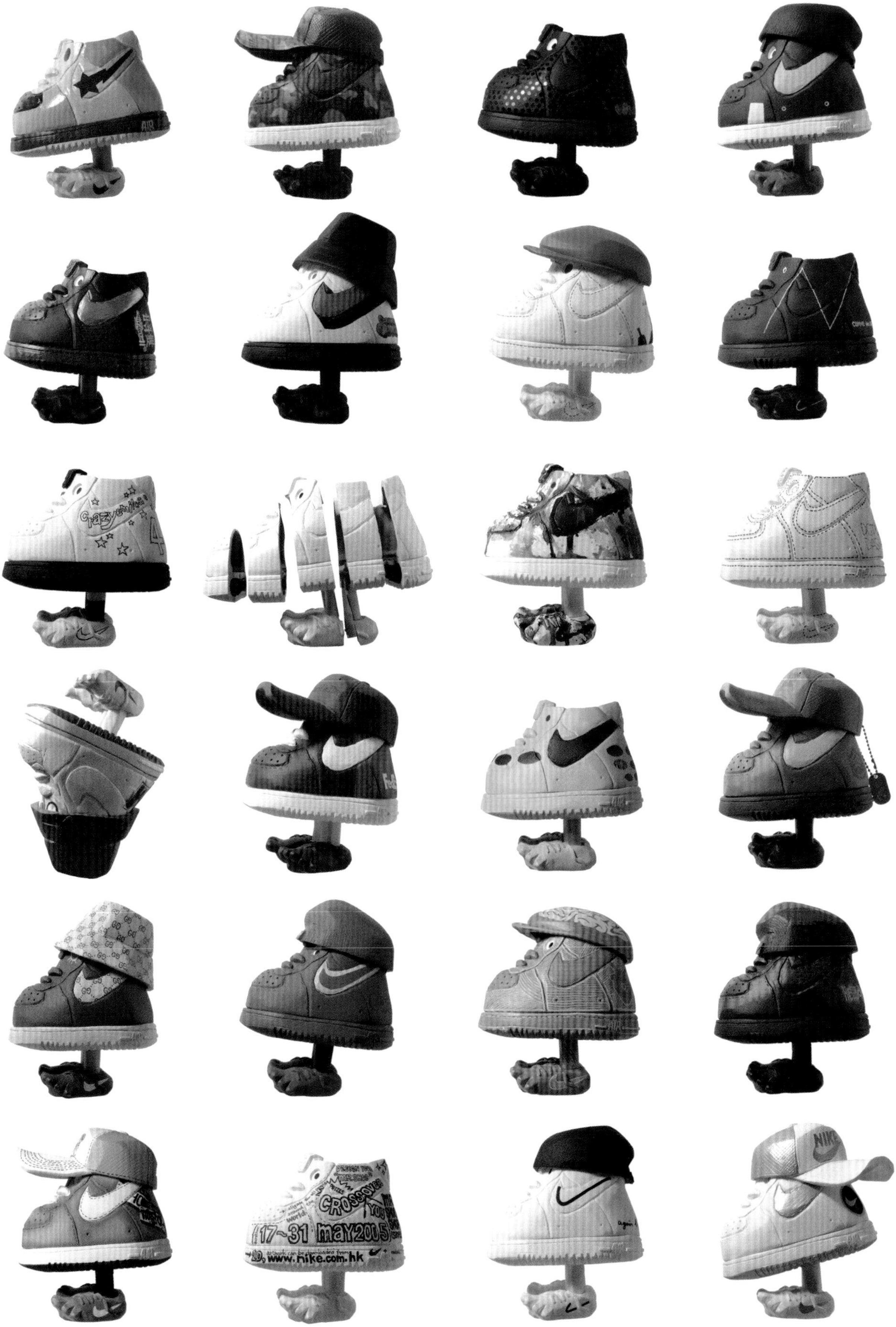

All images courtesy of maharishi

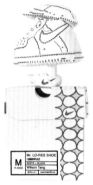

After a second show in Tokyo, fashion label maharishi brought the Mr. Shoe touring exhibition to the UK in 2005. Held at the DPMHI gallery in Soho, the exhibition featured all of Lau's Mr. Shoe pieces alongside one-off customized figures created by a range of leading designers and creatives, including Ben Drury, Eley Kishimoto, Zoltar and Lupe Fiasco. www.DPMHI.com

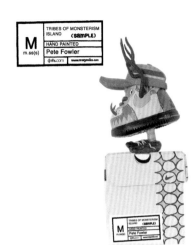

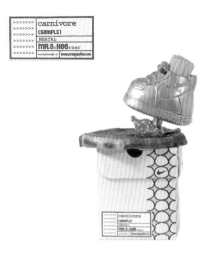

NIKE WILDWOOD

In 2002, Lau teamed up with designers FibreOps and Nike for the release of a limited-edition Wildwood sneaker. Limited to only 60 pairs worldwide, the shoes have 'FibreOps' embroidered on one shoe and 'Michael Lau' on the other.

As part of the release, Lau created this limited-edition Boy-D figure (part of Lau's Crazy Children series). The character has a pixelated face and is wearing a Nike shirt and hat – and is even sporting a miniature pair of the Nike Wildwood FibreOps shoes. The figure was limited to 540 pieces, comes with a Crazy Children pig (in one of two colours) and is packaged in a pixelated box. The version shown here is the maharishi variant, limited to just 100 pieces.

NIKE DUNK LOW SB

In 2006, Lau collaborated with Nike once again for the release of this wood-grain Dunk SB. Released in Hong Kong only, the shoe was limited to an edition of 106. Each pair came with a wooden box and a Michael Lau NY Fat wood-grain figure. Shown here is the friends-and-family version of the shoe created for Lau, featuring a number of differences including a detailed wood-grain midsole instead of the solid brown midsole on the Tier Zero release.

www.suite2206.com

JB CLASSICS LAB

The Bully is the first toy release under the JB Classics Lab division. Made from glass and standing 20cm high, the figure comes with two interchangeable sets of ceramic sneakers as well as a glass boombox.

The inspiration for the figure came from the sketchbooks of JB Classics founder Jason Bass. 'I've been illustrating daily now for 16 years,' says Bass. 'This particular character was coined The Bully. However, this Bully is a protector; he is the bully's bully.'

Fifty pieces were created, of which 25 were lost in production and only 18 were made available to retail. Those available were packaged in a hand-made, laser-etched and heat-stamped pine box.

www.amostoys.com

JAMES JARVIS

For the release of this Stüssy/Nike Court Force Low collaboration, illustrator and toy designer James Jarvis was asked to create a figure based on Stüssy's UK store manager Leon Dixon Goulden. 'I've known Leon for a good few years, and I had made a figure of him already for a set of capsule toys I had designed for Sony Creative Products in 2001. Dixon Goulden had remembered the toy and thought that a similar updated model wearing the Stüssy/Nike shoes would be a great promotional tool for the collaboration.'

According to Jarvis, making the toy was easy, given that he had already done the design work several years previously. 'I tried to avoid the temptation to tweak the original design too much, but I wanted to portray the judgmental aspect of Leon's personality, his generally intolerant nature.'

Inspired by fresh summer colours, the design of the shoes themselves was the responsibility of Steve Bryden, Leon Dixon Goulden and Mark Ward. Approximately 1000 pairs of sneakers (500 of each colour) and toys were produced.

Shown right: Stüssy store manager Leon Dixon Goulden was the inspiration for the figure. Jarvis also created a window display for the launch of the shoe at the London Stüssy store.

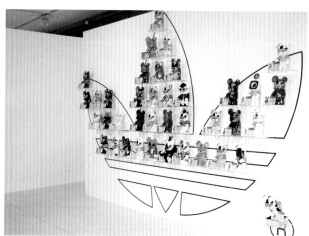

TOY2R DIY QEE EXHIBITION WITH ADICOLOR
Held in the adicolor studio at the Bread & Butter
trade show in Berlin, the exhibition featured adidas
Qee figures customized by selected international
artists and designers, including Tod McFarlane and
Gary Baseman. Shown below is Mr Set Letradidas
by Agathe Jacquillat and Tomi Vollauschek of
London-based design studio FI@33.

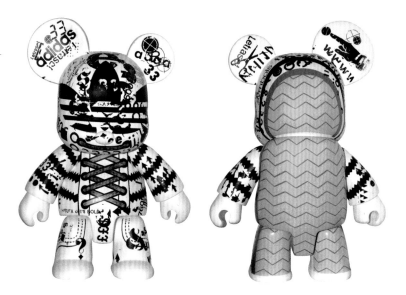

www.toy2r.com

TOY2R

Raymond Choy, president of Hong Kong-based Toy2r, opened his first toy store in 1995 after spending ten years working for a US footwear importer. Four years later, Choy decided to put all his funds into the development of his very first vinyl figure, the Toyer, and by 2001 he had developed the Qee Keychain collection, a uniquely designed keychain concept figure series.

In 2003 Toy2r collaborated with adidas by integrating a Qee figure with the adidas Superstar to make the adidas Qee (shown left). This collaboration was revisited in 2006 for the adidas adicolor launch exhibition, when more than 30 artists and designers from around the world were invited to customize an adidas Qee based on their adicolor inspiration.

ADICOLOR QEE SET
Launched in 2006, the adicolor Palette 5 sneaker collection (see page 108) was sold with one 6cm adicolor Qee in the same colour as the respective footwear model. Toy2r and adidas Originals also released a special limited-edition adicolor Qee pack consisting of seven coloured adicolor Qees plus one super-rare Trefoil Head adicolor Qee.

STORES

EUROPE

Colette
www.colette.fr

Dover Street Market
www.doverstreetmarket.com

Flatspot
www.flatspot.com

Foot Locker
www.footlocker.eu

Gloria's
www.superdeluxe.net

hanon Shop
www.hanon-shop.com

maharishi
www.dpmhi.com

Main Source
www.main-source.co.uk

90 Square Meters
www.90sqm.com

Nort
www.nortberlin.com

oki-ni
www.oki-ni.com

Opium
www.opiumstore.com

Overkill Berlin
www.overkillshop.com

Patta
www.teampatta.nl

Purchaze
www.purchaze.com

Shoeciety
www.shoeciety.com

Size?
www.size-online.com

sneakersnstuff
www.sneakersnstuff.com

Sold Out
www.wesoldout.com

Solebox
www.solebox.de

Starcow
www.starcow.net

Street Machine
www.streetmachine.fr

Stüssy
www.stussystore.co.uk

Trust Nobody
www.trustnobody.es

NORTH AMERICA

Alife
www.alifenyc.com

Bodega
www.bdgastore.com

Commonwealth
www.cmonwealth.com

Dave's Quality Meat
www.davesqualitymeat.com

Flight Club
www.flightclub.com

Goliath
www.goliathny.com

Good Foot
www.getonthegoodfoot.ca

HUF
www.hufsf.com

Instyleshoes
www.instyleshoes.com

Kidrobot
www.kidrobot.com

Livestock
www.deadstock.ca

Pick Your Shoes
www.pickyourshoes.com

Premium Goods
www.premiumgoods.net

Prodigy
www.prodigynyc.com

Proper
www.apropersite.com

Recon/Nort
www.reconstore.com

Richard Kidd
www.richardkidd.net

Solestop
www.solestop.com

Supreme
www.supremenewyork.com

Undefeated
undftd.com

ASIA/AUSTRALIA

Atmos
www.atmos-tokyo.com

Chapter World
www.chapterworld.com

Footage
www.footage.com.au

Mita
www.mita-sneakers.co.jp

Provider
www.provider.com.au

Sample Kickz
www.samplekickz.com

WEBSITES & BLOGS

Cliquenmove
www.cliquenmove.com

Cool Hunting
www.coolhunting.com

Crooked Tongues
www.cookedtongues.com

Fat Lace Magazine
www.fatlacemagazine.rawkus.com

Fecal Face
www.fecalface.com

5th Dimesion
www.5th-dimension.info

Fixins
www.fixins.com

Freshness Mag
www.freshnessmag.com

High Snobiety
www.highsnobiety.com

Honeyee
www.honeyee.com

Hypebeast
www.hypebeast.com

Juxtapoz
www.juxtapoz.com

Kix Files
www.kix-files.com

la mjc
www.lamjc.com

Lace magazine
www.lace-mag.de

New Balance Blog
www.newbalance-blog.com

New Kicks on the Blog
www.newkicksontheblog.com

Nike Talk
www.niketalk.com

Puma Talk
www.pumatalk.com

Slamxhype
www.slamxhype.com

Sneaker Freaker
www.sneakerfreaker.com

Sneaker Websites
www.sneaker-websites.com

Sole Collector
www.solecollector.com

ADIDAS
www.adidas.com

Brothers Adolph and Rudolph Dassler produced their first sports shoes in Herzogenaurach, Germany in 1920. Following a bitter feud, the two brothers parted company, with Rudolph going on to form Puma, while Adolph founded adidas. The adidas name dates back to 1948, deriving from the first three letters of Dassler's nickname (Adi) and his surname. One year later, Adi Dassler registered the Three Stripes as a trademark.

One of many breakthrough's for Dassler came when Germany won the Soccer World Cup in 1954. In the legendary final against Hungary, the German team wore boots with screw-in studs – made by adidas. Dassler also started using well-known athletes to endorse his products; the star-studded list including the likes of Jesse Owens, Muhammad Ali and Franz Beckenbauer.

Already associated with various subcultures such as reggae, the 1980s saw rap legends Run-DMC seal adidas' place in youth culture with the track 'My adidas'. The hip-hop act was known for their love of the adidas Superstar, which they would famously wear without laces.

Today, the adidas product range extends from shoes, apparel and accessories for basketball, football, fitness and training to adventure, trail and golf. The company is currently split into two main divisions, the first being Sports Performance, a range based on athletic performance and technological innovation, and the second being Sports Style, which is home to adidas Originals (a range of heritage and classic products) and Y-3 (the collaboration with Japanese fashion designer Yohji Yamamoto).

In 2006, the adidas Group acquired Reebok International, providing an even greater share of the global athletic footwear and apparel markets.

CONVERSE
www.converse.com

Marquis M. Converse opened the Converse Rubber Shoe Company (also known as the Boston Rubber Shoe Company) in Malden, Massachusetts in 1908. In 1915 the company began manufacturing canvas athletic shoes, but Converse's main turning point came in 1917 when the now legendary All-Star basketball shoe was introduced.

Then in 1921, Converse hired Charles H. 'Chuck' Taylor, a basketball player who had originally approached the company complaining of sore feet. He worked as a salesman and ambassador, promoting the All-Star shoes around the United States. In the 1930s his signature was added to the All Star patch. Also referred to as Cons, Connies, Chucks, or Chuckies, the Chuck Taylor All-Star basketball shoe originally only came in black or white. Under pressure from basketball teams it was decided in 1966 to manufacture other colours, and different materials also began to appear in the 1970s, such as suede and vinyl.

Although continuing to introduce new models, such as the Weapon and the All-Star Pro, Converse lost much of its monopoly on the professional courts from the 1980s onwards. This was largely the result of the surge of new competitors, such as Nike, who introduced radical new designs to the market. By the end of the 1990s Converse hit financial troubles and was subsequently purchased by Nike in 2003. Today, the company's roots remain firmly in basketball, and Converse supplies shoes to some of the NBA's top players, while still producing its classic designs for a much broader fanbase. As well as its sports heritage, Converse has always had close connections to subculture – from the birth of rock and roll and the youth rebellion that began in the 1950s, to punk rock and modern artists, performers and designers.

DEKLINE
www.dekline.com

Launched in 2004, San Diego-based Dekline produces a unique selection of skateboarding footwear and apparel. Since its inception, Dekline has had a strong history of collaboration, working with bands, artists, movies, DJs, photographers and even television shows. Part of Tum Yeto, the California-based skateboard distributor, Dekline also supports a skate team consisting of riders from the USA, France, Slovakia, New Zealand and Australia.

ETNIES
www.etnies.com

Established in 1986, Etnies is the first skateboarder-owned and operated global action sports footwear and apparel company. Founded in France, the brand's original name was Etnics, derived from the word ethnic - a reference to skateboarding subculture. Due to legal complications the name was changed to Etnies in 1987.

Etnies not only pushed the envelope by creating the first pro model skate shoe, but it also pioneered technological advances and changed the face of skateboard footwear forever.

Now based in California, Etnies' vision is to remain the leading action sports company committed to creating functional men's, women's and kid's footwear and apparel that provides the most style, comfort, durability and protection possible. Etnies stays true to its roots by sponsoring a world class team of skateboarding, surfing, snowboarding, moto-x and BMX athletes.

DC SHOES
www.dcshoes.com

Co-founded by Ken Block and Damon Way, DC Shoes began life in 1993. At the time, Block and Way had owned successful small clothing and snowboard outerwear companies Eightball, Dub and Droors Clothing (where the initials DC stem from). DC Shoes emerged from these brands and was officially born in 1994 when Damon's brother, professional skateboarder Danny Way, and his fellow pro Colin McKay agreed to leave their sponsors to represent the emerging shoe company.

DC Shoes was founded to create performance skateboarding shoes, and throughout its existence the company has introduced a number of technological and design innovations. These include abrasion-resistant materials (to help slow wear-and-tear caused by grip tape) and the use of elastic tongue-straps to secure a skateboarder's foot inside the shoe.

DC's product line now extends beyond skateboarding shoes. It includes casual and performance apparel, snowboards, snowboard boots, outerwear and accessories, as well as a full line of women's and kids' apparel, footwear and snowboarding outerwear and boots. As part of its marketing strategy, DC has also built a world-class team of professional skateboarding, snowboarding, surfing, BMX, motocross and rally athletes.

FEIYUE
www.feiyue-shoes.com

Feiyue (meaning 'flying forward') was born in Shanghai in 1920 and became known during the 1930s for their shoe's robustness, flexibility and comfort – later becoming the essential footwear for Chinese martial artists.

In 2006 Patrice Bastian and Charles Munka, founders of the Seven Dice collective, decided to team up with Feiyue to relaunch and give a whole new identity to the brand.

Influenced by their personal experiences and world travels, Seven Dice now create all Feiyue's collections. The collective works closely with the Feiyue factory, which still uses manufacturing processes from 1905 – with unique ovens used to mould the vulcanized Feiyue outsoles. The entire assembly process for each shoe is completed by hand.

GRAVIS
www.gravisfootwear.com

Founded in Burlington, Vermont in 1998, Gravis Footwear has been making quality sneakers for over a decade. Gravis grew out of the Burton Snowboarding company and maintains its ties to the action sports community with its design aesthetic. Bridging the gap between pure sport function and casual style, Gravis takes the best features, materials and construction techniques from pure athletic shoes (like skate, running and hiking), and incorporates them into shoes with a clean, modern look. Working closely with a team of professional snowboarders, surfers, musicians and artists, Gravis develops shoes, bags and accessories for today's active lifestyle.

Gravis has always focused on product research, development and attention to detail in an effort to produce forward-thinking and original products. In 2001 the groundbreaking (limited-edition) artist collaboration foot bed series marked the beginning of the Gravis Perimeter Support Foot bed system.

JB CLASSICS
www.suite2206.com

Launched in San Francisco in 2001 as a reaction to founder Jason Bass' disillusionment with the contemporary footwear industry, JB Classics is a footwear and lifestyle brand with its roots in streetwear, sport, design, art and entertainment.

In late 2004, Bass and designer Mdot joined forces to create JB Classics Lab®. Focused on design, JB Classics Lab® incorporates the comfort of an athletic sneaker with the aesthetic and detail of a luxury shoe, mixing premium materials with strong and vibrant colour combinations.

LACOSTE
www.lacoste.com

After helping to steal the Davis Cup away from the Americans for the first time in 1927, René Lacoste earned himself the nickname The Alligator – partly over a bet concerning an alligator-skin suitcase, and partly from the tenacity with which he played tennis. Shortly after this, Lacoste had a crocodile embroidered onto the back of the blazer he wore on the courts.

In 1933, Lacoste and André Gillier, the owner and president of the largest French knitwear-manufacturing firm of that time, set up a company to manufacture shirts embroidered with Lacoste's crocodile logo. It is believed to be the first time a logo appeared on the outside of a garment. The shirt revolutionized men's sportswear and replaced the starched long-sleeved classic shirts.

In 1985 the Lacoste brand launched a new line of tennis shoes, manufactured in France, followed by deck shoes in 1986 and walking shoes in 1988. Since then the company has vastly expanded its range of sneakers, while keeping its heritage firmly planted in the world of tennis.

LAKAI
www.lakai.com

In 1993, Mike Carroll and Rick Howard thought they might have a better formula for a skateboard company – one that made products the team would be proud of and kept an atmosphere that was supportive and motivating. While it was a risk, they felt like they owed it to skateboarding and skateboarders to take that risk and co-founded Chocolate/Girl Skateboards.

In 1999, facing a similar situation in respect to footwear, Mike and Rick introduced Lakai Limited Footwear with the same dedication and pride they invested into their skateboarding and the Girl/Chocolate brands.

Lakai is based in Torrance, California and represented by Rick Howard, Mike Carroll, Eric Koston, Marc Johnson, Guy Mariano, Cairo Foster, Brandon Biebel, Jeff Lenoce, Rob Welsh, Mike Mo Capaldi, Vincent Alvarez, Jesus Fernandez, The French Connection and The Royal Family.

MADFOOT
www.madfoot.jp

Founded by designer Takashi Imai in 2001, Madfoot is a Japanese brand born from an obsession with sneakers. Producing products that are simply what the Madfoot team wants to wear, the company is known for concentrating on the subtle details of their footwear designs. A great example is the Madfoot collaboration with Saucony, where the colourful appendages of the sneaker were actually based on a wrestling mask wrapping around the shoe – and tracing the outline of selected panels on the shoe reveal the word 'mad'.

NEW BALANCE
www.newbalance.com

New Balance was founded at the dawn of the twentieth century in Boston, Massachusetts when William J. Riley, a 33-year-old English immigrant, began to help people with problematic feet by making arch supports and prescription footwear. In 1934, Riley went into partnership with his leading salesman, Arthur Hall – who had been highly successful selling arch supports to policemen and other people who were on their feet all day. In 1954, Hall sold the business to his daughter and son-in-law, Eleanor and Paul Kidd. Arch supports and prescription footwear remained the cornerstone of their business until 1961 when they manufactured The Trackster, the world's first performance running shoe made with a ripple sole and available in multiple widths.

During the 1960s New Balance's reputation for manufacturing innovative performance footwear available in multiple widths grew from word of mouth. On the day of the Boston Marathon in 1972, Jim Davis bought the company and, joined by Anne Davis in 1977, committed themselves to upholding the company's founding values of comfort and performance. To this day, New Balance adheres to a unique set of philosophies: focusing on function by making shoes in multiple widths, continuing to take an 'endorsed by no one' stance, and by manufacturing a large percentage of its shoes with a high-quality labour force.

NIKE
www.nike.com

The biggest of all the footwear brands, and certainly the most prolific when it comes to collaborating, Nike was founded by Phil Knight, a University of Oregon business student and middle-distance runner, and Bill Bowerman, the legendary University of Oregon track and field coach.

Knight and Bowerman shared the ambition of importing high-quality, yet affordable, Japanese running shoes to the US. After completing his studies in 1962, Knight departed on a trip around the world. One of his many stops was Japan, where he contacted Onitsuka Tiger, convincing the company of the great marketing opportunities for its product in the US. Put on the spot to appear as though he owned a company, Knight made up a company name, giving birth to Blue Ribbon Sports, the forerunner of Nike. In 1964 Knight and Bowerman joined together in this new enterprise, each agreeing to contribute US$500 to the partnership. The first shipment of 300 pairs of Tiger running shoes sold out within three weeks.

Although the company rapidly gained in reputation, it didn't take long before Bowerman was looking for new ways to improve the performance of the shoes, and Knight was thinking about how much more profitable it would be for them to produce the shoes themselves.

In 1971 Jeff Johnson, Nike's first employee, made his most enduring contribution to the company; while sleeping he dreamt of Nike, the Greek goddess of victory – giving Blue Ribbon Sports the name for its first piece of footwear. In the same year, for a fee of $35, graphic design student Carolyn Davidson created the Swoosh trademark.

A distribution dispute led to an eventual break in business relations between BRS and Onitsuka Tiger in 1972 – the same year as the Nike Moon Shoes debuted at the US Olympic trials. By 1974 The Waffle Trainer was introduced, featuring Bowerman's famous Waffle outsole; an infamous experiment that Bowerman had conducted by pouring a liquid rubber compound into his wife's waffle iron. It quickly became the best-selling training shoe in the country.

Since then Nike has continued to innovate and dominate in the footwear industry. In 1979 Nike created the first Air-Sole units, one of the greatest footwear cushioning innovations ever developed. The company introduced the Tailwind in early 1979 (the first running shoe with the patented Air-Sole cushioning system) and the Air Force 1 basketball shoe in 1982 (the first Nike basketball shoe to incorporate a Nike Air cushion). The first Air Jordan basketball shoes debuted in 1985 (endorsed by Chicago Bulls basketball rookie Michael Jordan, who was famously fined thousands of dollars per game for continually breaking the NBA's white footwear policy by wearing the red and black Air Jordan 1), and 1987 saw the launch of the groundbreaking Air Max 1 (designed by Tinker Hatfield, this was the first shoe to make the Nike Air technology visible). Much more has followed, including the recent technological innovations of Nike Free barefoot running and the Nike Air Max 360 foamless midsole.

Nike currently employs approximately 29,000 people, operating on six continents with suppliers, shippers, retailers and service providers totalling almost one million people.

ONITSUKA TIGER
www.onitsukatiger.com

In 1949, Kihachiro Onitsuka established Onitsuka Tiger, with a philosophy of promoting youth health through sports. Regular consultation with sportsmen and their coaches helped him to make the best sports shoes in Japan. Famously, in 1951, during a vacation Onitsuka saw a plate with pickles and octopus legs. He realized that the suction cups of the octopus could be the key to grip, and used the concept for the sole of the basketball shoes he was working on at the time.

The brand continues today as part of ASICS. Based on the original sports shoes, Onitsuka Tiger combines its unique Japanese heritage with contemporary design – twenty-five years of sports experience has been fused with Japanese tradition to create a collection of footwear and apparel.

POINTER
www.pointerfootwear.com

Gareth Skewis and Rose Choules established Pointer in 2004. Based in London, the company was created with the aim of making simple, well-designed casual shoes. Pointer employs people it likes and the company is backed by a creative stable of friends and collaborators (including artists/designers Nik Taylor, Jethro Haynes, Marcus Oakley, French and Hudson-Powell), inspired and informed by everything from art to music and skateboarding.

PUMA
www.puma.com

The Gebrüder Dassler Schuhfabrik footwear company was started in 1924 in Herzogenaurach, Germany. The name Puma wasn't introduced until 1948, with the formation of Puma Schuhfabrik Rudolf Dassler. The brand was started by Rudolph Dassler – brother of Adi, the founder of adidas. After World War II, during which Rudolph Dassler had spent time in a POW camp, the Dassler brothers began a legendary feud, causing Rudolph to split from his brother and found Puma. This led to an intense battle between Puma and adidas to get their shoes onto the feet of world-class athletes – something that saw Puma sponsoring sporting greats such as football legend Pele and tennis superstar Boris Becker.

The Puma formstripe was introduced in 1956, not as a branding exercise, but as a way of adding strength and stability to the shoes. The introduction of the modern cat logo wasn't until 1968.

Alongside sports, Puma heritage is deeply rooted in the subcultures of hip-hop and skateboarding. In fact, skaters in the early 1990s wore Puma Suedes and Baskets, a relationship that Puma has since developed with the launch of a specifically-designed skateboard shoe.

Although probably best loved for their classic designs such as the Clyde and State, Puma have constantly been at the forefront of technical innovation –; introducing such advances as the Trinomic shock-absorption technology (1989) and the Puma Disc closure system (1991). The company has also been successful in expanding into niche markets like motor sports and continues to collaborate with some of the world's top designers including Philippe Starck, Alexander McQueen and Yasuhiro Mihara.

REEBOK
www.reebok.com

In the 1890s, UK-based Joseph William Foster made some of the first-known spiked running shoes. By 1895, he was in business making shoes by hand for top runners, and before long his fledgling company, J.W. Foster and Sons, had developed an international clientele of distinguished athletes.

In 1958, two of the founder's grandsons, Jeff and Joe Foster, started a companion company that came to be known as Reebok, named after an African gazelle. In 1979, Paul Fireman, a partner in an outdoor sporting goods distributorship, spotted Reebok shoes at an international trade show and negotiated for the North American distribution licence. The company then introduced a small range of running shoes (at US$60, they were the most expensive running shoes on the market) to the US at the end of the 1970s.

Reebok are most famed for capitalizing on the aerobics phenomenon of the 1980s, introducing the Freestyle, the company's best-selling athletic shoe of all time, in 1982. Explosive growth followed, fuelled by Reebok extending further into other sporting areas and expanding into overseas markets. In the late 1980s, a particularly successful period began with introduction of Pump technology – inflatable air chambers on the inside of the shoes enabling a custom fit.

In the late 1990s, Reebok made a strategic commitment to align its brand with a select few of the world's most talented athletes, including basketball star Allen Iverson and tennis ace Venus Williams. Reebok have also formed partnerships with the NFL and the NBA.

In 2002, Reebok launched Rbk – a collection of street-inspired footwear and apparel collaborations, including the G-Unit collection and the S. Carter (Jay-Z) collection. Reebok is now owned by the German footwear giant adidas-Salomon, which completed its acquisition in 2006.

VANS
www.vans.com

Based in Southern California, Vans was founded in 1966 by Paul Van Doren. Originally known as the Van Doren Rubber Company, all shoes were created using the vulcanized rubber method – involving bonding the rubber to the canvas of the shoe in huge ovens. The results gave the shoes a very hard rubber sole, ideal for skateboarding or BMX.

In the early days of the company (pre-empting manufactured sneaker customization by decades), Vans made their shoes to order. Customers could order a pair of shoes in the colour or fabric of their choice – they could even supply their own fabric if desired.

In the 1980s, Vans lost much of its core customer base when the company started trying to expand its market – developing shoes for everything from running to wrestling, and the corporation was forced into bankruptcy protection. The company survived its financial troubles and was back on track by 1989 with the introduction of the first skateboarding signature shoe, The Cab, for Steve Caballero.

Vans continues to develop new models, such as the best-selling Rowley XLT, alongside its classic shoe designs.

CONVERSE ONE
www.converse.com

The Converse One custom website allows the user to create and personalize their own shoe designs, offering a choice of models, including the Chuck Taylor All Star hi-top, low-top, slip or SkidGrip. Each shoe has varying colour choices and even a selection of patterns to choose from (such as tribal skulls and fingerprints). Other nice touches are the ability to select contrast stitching (a detail that is overlooked by other custom sites) and the ability to choose the typeface (Arial or Corsiva) for the personalization aspect of the shoe. The interface itself (including the audio elements) is almost identical to the Nike iD site.

NIKEiD
www.nikeid.com

Incredibly, Nike has been offering its iD concept to the public since 1999, allowing consumers to custom-order footwear via the Internet in various colour combinations and with a personal message (as long as it is between three and ten characters long). The concept began with just two models and a total of 84 possible colour combinations. Since then, the range of models (now including clothing and accessories), colours and materials has grown considerably.

In addition to this online service, Nike opened its first iD studio space in 2005 – an exclusive New York boutique where the only way to gain access was to be invited. Studios in Paris, Berlin and London soon followed – with little publicity. Unassuming from the outside, the modernist design of these exclusive and luxury boutiques housed specially-commissioned artwork, vintage sneakers and various blank display models and colour swatches to help with the design process.

Nike has now expanded this concept even further by opening iD studios in a number of their Niketown stores worldwide. To gain entry to these public studios users must book an appointment with one of several design consultants, each of whom has a background in graphic design or fashion. The studios feature a larger range of shoes than online, plus exclusive models (which change roughly every season) and a bigger choice of materials, including crinkled patent, patent, perforated, smooth, mock crocodile and mock snakeskin.

RBKCUSTOM
www.rbkcustom.com

The amount of detail and colour/material choice available at Reebok's custom site is very impressive. Launched in 2005, the site features a great interface that allows the user to toggle views – from the straightforward image of a shoe, to a view of the shoe actually being worn. Also, when commencing a design, it is possible to choose from example shoes designed by previous users of the site (as well as a blank shoe option).

Models currently available on the site include the Classic Leather, Freestyle, League (NFL and MLB teams), Ventilator, Supercourt, Daddy Yankee and the DJ II. The site was US-only, but will be launching in Europe during 2008. The site also hosts the release of limited-edition Reebok shoes.

MY ETNIES
me.etnies.com

Using illustrations instead of photographic images of the shoes, the My Etnies site has an intentionally DIY quality. Currently only available in the US, the site offers a range of six shoes, the Team 1, the Sheckler, the Dropout, the Capital, the Easy-E and the Callicut. My Etnies offers the consumer several colour choices, a selection of patterns (such as gingham and the ever-popular skull design) and additional personalization options.

PUMA MONGOLIAN SHOE BBQ
www.mongolianshoebbq.puma.com

Puma's Mongolian Shoe BBQ gives consumers a tactile shoe-making experience. Using the style of Mongolian Barbecue cuisine as the recipe for the program, customers can design their own shoe from an assortment of pre-cut fabrics. Thirteen components and detailing can be customized from a wide variety of materials and fabrics.

At selected Puma stores, customers can assemble their shoe at a specially designed fixture in keeping with the barbecue theme. A refrigerator display case houses examples for inspiration and sizing. The workspace incorporates the pattern of the shoe to use as a guide, along with recipe instructions for the creative process. Various pattern pieces can then be selected from the component buffet and scanned into a computer, and a rendering of the finished product can be previewed at the workstation.

The online program uses the same basic 'cooking' experience. A virtual Mongolian BBQ restaurant has been created to take users through the sneaker buffet and the finished product is displayed in a 3D rendering. The finished sneakers are shipped within five to six weeks.

VANS CUSTOM
www.shop.vans.com

Vans famously began making shoes to order in the 1960s when customers could order a pair of shoes in the colour or fabric of their choice directly from the factory. This (US only) website is today's equivalent of that concept and offers a generous colour and pattern choice (including Vans' signature checkerboard pattern). The two models available for customization are the Slip-On and the Old Skool.

ACKNOWLEDGEMENTS:
Intercity would like to thank all the artists and
designers featured in this book, and to also give
thanks to those people behind the scenes who
helped make this project happen, including
Mark Bodé, Thomas Peiser, Chloe Longstaff,
Robeson Mueller, Charlie Morgan and all at
Crooked Tongues, Jason Bass, Joanna Sieghart,
Merryl Spence, Louisa Hammond, Karmen Wjinberg,
Pat Lo, Jose Cabaco, Helen Sweeney-Dougan,
Alison Day, Gary Aspden, Michael Klein, Chris Law,
Jess Weinstein, Lauren Kauffman, Kristina Helb,
Matt Ting, Brian Lynn, Shirley Schlatka, Allie Emery,
Jason Thome, Keith Gulla, Nick Street,
Victoria Barrio, Chris Overholser, August Benzien,
Eladio Correa, Ashton Maxfield, Cristina Kown,
Ashley Roberts, Daniel Glover, Helen Crossley,
Barbara Normile, Penny Keen, Gareth Skewis,
Peter Stitson, Rosina Budhani, Giorgio de Mitri,
Manuel Maggio, Simon Porter, Joris Pol, Chris Love,
Damian Loiselle, James Lavelle, Mubi, Jesse Leyva,
Jill Meisner, Drieke Leenknegt, Nate Tobecksen,
Jason Badden, Mark Rhodes, Leo Sandino-Taylor,
Acyde, Sebastian Palmer, Natsuhiko Kubota,
Jun Shigenobu, Kasei JJ Lin, Masahiko Yamazaki,
Kojiro, John Benson, Mark Ward, Peter Glanvill,
Gavin Lucas, Donald Dinwiddie, Jo Lightfoot,
and the FBRS.

Thanks also to PSC Photography, Anna Purchall
and Lee Hind for their help with photography.

A special thanks to Emma (who also thought of the
title of this book) and Stanley for their endless
support and inspiration throughout the difficult
times surrounding the production of Art & Sole.
I love you both. NG